Complete
low-carb
COOKBOOK

Publications International, Ltd.

Favorite Brand Name Recipes at www.fbnr.com

Pictured on the front cover: Mesquite-Grilled Salmon Fillet *(page 100)*.
Pictured on the back cover *(top to bottom):* Pozole *(page 76)* and Strawberry-Topped Cheesecake Cups *(page 178)*.

ISBN: 1-4127-2090-7

Library of Congress Control Number: 2004106043

Manufactured in China.

8 7 6 5 4 3 2 1

Nutritional Analysis: The nutritional information that appears with each recipe was submitted in part by the participating companies and associations. Every effort has been made to check the accuracy of these numbers. However, because numerous variables account for a wide range of values for certain foods, nutritive analyses in this book should be considered approximate.

Microwave Cooking: Microwave ovens vary in wattage. Use the cooking times as guidelines and check for doneness before adding more time.

Preparation/Cooking Times: Preparation times are based on the approximate amount of time required to assemble the recipe before cooking, baking, chilling or serving. These times include preparation steps such as measuring, chopping and mixing. The fact that some preparations and cooking can be done simultaneously is taken into account. Preparation of optional ingredients and serving suggestions is not included.

Note: This book is for informational purposes and is not intended to provide medical advice. Neither Publications International, Ltd., nor the authors, editors or publisher take responsibility for any possible consequences from any treatment, procedure, exercise, dietary modification, action, or applications of medication or preparation by any person reading or following the information in this cookbook. The publication of this book does not constitute the practice of medicine, and this cookbook does not attempt to replace your physician or your pharmacist. **Before undertaking any course of treatment, the authors, editors and publisher advise the reader to check with a physician or other health care provider.**

table of contents

Nibbling Nosh

Spicy Shrimp Cocktail

Prep Time: 6 minutes   *Cook Time:* 10 minutes

> **2 tablespoons olive or vegetable oil**
> **¼ cup finely chopped onion**
> **1 tablespoon chopped green bell pepper**
> **1 clove garlic, minced**
> **1 can (8 ounces) CONTADINA® Tomato Sauce**
> **1 tablespoon chopped pitted green olives, drained**
> **¼ teaspoon red pepper flakes**
> **1 pound cooked shrimp, chilled**

1. Heat oil in small skillet. Add onion, bell pepper and garlic; sauté until vegetables are tender. Stir in tomato sauce, olives and red pepper flakes.

2. Bring to a boil; simmer, uncovered, for 5 minutes. Cover.

3. Chill thoroughly. Combine sauce with shrimp in small bowl.   *Makes 6 servings*

Note: Serve over mixed greens, if desired.

NUTRIENTS PER SERVING (⅙ of total recipe without mixed greens):
Carbohydrate: 3 g, Fat: 6 g, Protein: 17 g, Calories: 129 (39% of calories from fat), Saturated Fat: 1 g, Sodium: 402 mg

Carpaccio di Zucchini

Prep and Cook Time: 28 minutes

¾ **pound zucchini, shredded**
½ **cup sliced almonds, toasted**
1 **tablespoon prepared Italian dressing**
4 **French bread baguettes, sliced in half lengthwise**
4 **teaspoons soft-spread margarine**
3 **tablespoons grated Parmesan cheese**
  Cherry tomatoes, halved, for garnish

1. Preheat broiler. Place zucchini in medium bowl. Add almonds and dressing; mix well. Set aside.

2. Place baguette halves on large baking sheet; spread evenly with margarine. Sprinkle with cheese. Broil 3 inches from heat 2 to 3 minutes or until edges and cheese are browned.

3. Spread zucchini mixture evenly on each baguette half. Garnish with cherry tomato halves, if desired. Serve immediately.   *Makes 4 servings*

NUTRIENTS PER SERVING (¼ of total recipe): Carbohydrate: 14 g, Fat: 15 g, Protein: 7 g, Calories: 207 (61% of calories from fat), Saturated Fat: 2 g, Sodium: 263 mg

Adobo Chicken Wings

Prep Time: 15 minutes   *Cook Time:* 50 minutes

18 chicken wings (about 3 pounds)
2 teaspoons LAWRY'S® Lemon Pepper
1 tablespoon LAWRY'S® Garlic Powder With Parsley
1 tablespoon onion powder
1 tablespoon ground cumin
1 tablespoon ground coriander
1 tablespoon Spanish paprika
1 teaspoon ground allspice
½ cup CARB OPTIONS™ Whipped Dressing
½ tablespoon TABASCO® (or to taste)

1. Preheat oven to 425°F. Cut the tips off the chicken wings; cut wings in half at the joint. In a large bowl, combine the dry seasonings; stir in wings.

2. On a baking pan, arrange wings. Bake 50 minutes or until thoroughly cooked. Broil, if desired, for extra crispness.

3. In a large bowl, blend Carb Options Whipped Dressing and Tabasco. Toss cooked wings in sauce until evenly coated and serve.   *Makes 9 servings*

NUTRIENTS PER SERVING (2 to 3 wings): Carbohydrate: 3 g, Fat: 27 g, Protein: 31 g, Calories: 390 (62% of calories from fat), Saturated Fat: 7 g, Sodium: 260 mg

So-Low-Carb Appetizer

Prep Time: 8 minutes   *Cook Time:* 14 minutes   *Cool Time:* 15 minutes

Nonstick cooking spray
1 large red bell pepper, cut into 1-inch pieces
1 large yellow squash, sliced into ¼-inch-thick rounds
1 medium onion, quartered and layers separated
1 tablespoon olive oil
1½ teaspoons balsamic vinegar
½ teaspoon dried basil leaves
¼ teaspoon salt

1. Preheat oven to 475°F.

2. Line baking sheet with foil; spray with cooking spray. Arrange vegetables in single layer on baking sheet. Spray vegetables with cooking spray. Roast 14 minutes or until vegetables begin to brown on edges. Do not stir.

3. Remove baking sheet from oven; place on wire rack to cool.

4. Combine oil, vinegar, basil and salt in small bowl. Drizzle over vegetables.

Makes 4 servings

NUTRIENTS PER SERVING (½ cup): Carbohydrate: 6 g, Fat: 4 g, Protein: 1 g, Calories: 60 (60% of calories from fat), Saturated Fat: <1 g, Sodium: 150 mg

Roasted Garlic Spread with Three Cheeses

2 medium heads garlic
2 packages (8 ounces each) fat-free cream cheese, softened
1 package (3½ ounces) goat cheese
2 tablespoons (1 ounce) crumbled blue cheese
1 teaspoon dried thyme leaves
   Fresh thyme and red bell pepper strip, for garnish (optional)
   Assorted cut-up vegetables for dipping

1. Preheat oven to 400°F. Cut tops off garlic heads to expose tops of cloves. Place garlic in small baking pan; bake 45 minutes or until garlic is very tender. Remove from pan; cool completely. Squeeze garlic into small bowl; mash with fork.

2. Beat cream cheese and goat cheese in small bowl until smooth; stir in blue cheese, garlic and thyme. Cover; refrigerate 3 hours or overnight.

3. Spoon dip into serving bowl; serve with cucumbers, radishes, carrots, yellow bell peppers or crackers, if desired. Garnish with fresh thyme and red bell pepper strip, if desired.   *Makes 21 servings*

NUTRIENTS PER SERVING (2 tablespoons spread without dippers):
Carbohydrate: 2 g, Fat: 1 g, Protein: 4 g, Calories: 37 (29% of calories from fat), Saturated Fat: <1 g, Sodium: 157 mg

Roasted Garlic Spread with Three Cheeses

Baked Spinach Balls

2 cups sage and onion or herb-seasoned bread stuffing mix
1 small onion, chopped
2 tablespoons grated Parmesan cheese
1 clove garlic, minced
¼ teaspoon dried thyme leaves
¼ teaspoon black pepper
1 package (10 ounces) frozen chopped spinach, thawed and squeezed dry
¼ cup fat-free reduced-sodium chicken broth
2 egg whites, beaten
Dijon or honey mustard (optional)

1. Combine bread stuffing mix, onion, cheese, garlic, thyme and pepper in medium bowl; mix well. Combine spinach, broth and egg whites in separate medium bowl; mix well. Stir into bread cube mixture. Cover; refrigerate 1 hour or until mixture is firm.

2. Preheat oven to 350°F. Shape mixture into 24 balls. Place on ungreased baking sheet; bake 15 minutes or until spinach balls are browned. Serve with mustard for dipping, if desired. *Makes 12 servings*

NUTRIENTS PER SERVING (2 spinach balls without mustard): Carbohydrate: 9 g, Fat: 1 g, Protein: 3 g, Calories: 52 (12% of calories from fat), Saturated Fat: <1 g, Sodium: 227 mg

Baked Spinach Balls

Salmon and Crab Cakes

8 ounces cooked salmon
8 ounces cooked crab
1 beaten egg *or* ¼ cup egg substitute
1½ tablespoons reduced-fat mayonnaise
1 tablespoon minced fresh parsley
1 teaspoon dried dill weed
½ teaspoon salt substitute
½ teaspoon black pepper
½ teaspoon mustard
¼ teaspoon low-sodium Worcestershire sauce
¼ cup bread crumbs
Nonstick cooking spray

1. Flake salmon and crab meat together in a medium mixing bowl. Add egg, mayonnaise, parsley, dill, salt substitute, pepper, mustard and Worcestershire sauce. Mix well.

2. Place bread crumbs on a shallow rimmed plate. Drop heaping ⅓ cup fish mixture into bread crumbs; shape into thick patty. Repeat with remaining mixture.

3. Spray large nonstick skillet with cooking spray; heat over medium heat. Cover; cook fish cakes 5 to 8 minutes, turning once. *Makes 4 fish cakes*

NUTRIENTS PER SERVING (1 fish cake): Carbohydrate: 5 g, Fat: 6 g, Protein: 24 g, Calories: 175 (33% of calories from fat), Saturated Fat: <1 g, Sodium: 736 mg

Feta-Stuffed Tomatoes

Prep Time: 5 minutes

2 small roma tomatoes (about ¼ pound)
⅓ cup seeded and chopped cucumber
1 tablespoon crumbled reduced-fat feta cheese
1 tablespoon fat-free sour cream
1 tablespoon chopped fresh mint
½ teaspoon finely grated lemon peel
¼ teaspoon black pepper

1. Cut tomatoes lengthwise into halves. Scoop out and discard pulp, leaving ¼-inch-thick shells. Place tomato shells, cut-side down, on paper towels to drain.

2. Combine cucumber, feta cheese, sour cream, mint, lemon peel, and pepper in small bowl. Spoon mixture into tomato shells. *Makes 4 servings*

NUTRIENTS PER SERVING (1 stuffed tomato half): Carbohydrate: 2 g, Fat: 1 g, Protein: 1 g, Calories: 17 (30% of calories from fat), Saturated Fat: <1 g, Sodium: 34 mg

Jicama & Shrimp Cocktail with Roasted Red Pepper Sauce

  2 large red bell peppers
  6 ounces (about 24 medium-large) shrimp, peeled and deveined
  1 medium clove garlic
1½ cups fresh cilantro sprigs
  2 tablespoons lime juice
  2 tablespoons orange juice
  ½ teaspoon hot pepper sauce
  1 small jicama (about ¾ pound), peeled and cut into strips
  1 plum tomato, halved, seeded and thinly sliced

1. Place bell peppers on broiler pan. Broil 4 to 6 inches from heat about 6 minutes, turning every 2 to 3 minutes or until all sides are charred. Transfer peppers to paper bag; close bag tightly. Let stand 10 minutes or until peppers are cool enough to handle and skins are loosened. Peel peppers; cut in half. Remove cores, seeds and membranes; discard.

2. Add shrimp to large saucepan of boiling water. Reduce heat to medium-low; simmer, uncovered, 2 to 3 minutes or until shrimp turn pink. Drain shrimp; rinse under cold running water. Cover; refrigerate until ready to use.

3. Place peppers and garlic in food processor; process until peppers are coarsely chopped. Add cilantro, lime juice, orange juice and pepper sauce; process until cilantro is finely chopped but mixture is not puréed.

4. Combine jicama, shrimp and tomato in large bowl. Add bell pepper mixture; toss to coat evenly. Serve over lettuce.   *Makes 8 servings*

NUTRIENTS PER SERVING (3 shrimp): Carbohydrate: 10 g, Fat: 1 g, Protein: 6 g, Calories: 69 (7% of calories from fat), Saturated Fat: <1 g, Sodium: 120 mg

Jicama & Shrimp Cocktail with Roasted Red Pepper Sauce

Cheddar Cheese and Rice Roll

Prep Time: 20 minutes   *Cook Time:* none

2 cups cooked UNCLE BEN'S® ORIGINAL CONVERTED® Brand Rice
3 cups grated low-fat Cheddar cheese
¾ cup fat-free cream cheese, softened
1 can (4½ ounces) green chilies, drained, chopped
⅛ teaspoon hot sauce
1½ cups chopped walnuts

PREP: CLEAN: Wash hands. Combine rice, Cheddar cheese, cream cheese, chilies and hot sauce. Mix by hand or in food processor. Shape mixture into a log. Roll in walnuts. Wrap tightly with plastic wrap and refrigerate 1 hour.

SERVE: Serve with assorted crackers.

CHILL: Refrigerate leftovers immediately.   *Makes 15 servings*

NUTRIENTS PER SERVING (about ½ cup): Carbohydrate: 10 g, Fat: 10 g,
Protein: 11 g, Calories: 168 (52% of calories from fat), Saturated Fat: 2 g, Sodium: 260 mg

Cheddar Cheese and Rice Roll

Savory Zucchini Sticks

Nonstick olive oil cooking spray
3 tablespoons seasoned dry bread crumbs
2 tablespoons grated Parmesan cheese
1 egg white
1 teaspoon reduced-fat (2%) milk
2 small zucchini (about 4 ounces each), cut lengthwise into quarters
⅓ cup spaghetti sauce, warmed

1. Preheat oven to 400°F. Spray baking sheet with cooking spray; set aside.

2. Combine bread crumbs and Parmesan cheese in shallow dish. Combine egg white and milk in another shallow dish; beat with fork until well blended.

3. Dip each zucchini wedge first into crumb mixture, then into egg white mixture, letting excess drip back into dish. Roll again in crumb mixture to coat.

4. Place zucchini sticks on prepared baking sheet; coat well with cooking spray. Bake 15 to 18 minutes or until golden brown. Serve with spaghetti sauce.   *Makes 4 servings*

NUTRIENTS PER SERVING (2 sticks with 1 tablespoon plus 1 teaspoon spaghetti sauce): Carbohydrate: 9 g, Fat: 2 g, Protein: 4 g, Calories: 69 (26% of calories from fat), Saturated Fat: 1 g, Sodium: 329 mg

Savory Zucchini Sticks

Hot or Cold Tuna Snacks

4 ounces light cream cheese
1 can (6 ounces) water-packed chunk light tuna, well drained
1 tablespoon chopped fresh parsley
1 tablespoon minced onion
½ teaspoon dried oregano leaves
½ teaspoon black pepper
18 (½-inch-thick) slices seedless cucumber
18 capers, for garnish (optional)

1. Combine cream cheese, tuna, parsley, onion, oregano and pepper in medium bowl; mix well.

2. Mound about 1 tablespoon tuna mixture to completely cover top of each cucumber slice. If serving cold, garnish with capers, if desired.

3. To serve hot, preheat oven to 500°F. Spray baking sheet with nonstick cooking spray. Place snacks on prepared baking sheet and bake 10 minutes or until tops are puffed and brown. Garnish with capers, if desired.   *Makes 6 servings*

Note: Capers are the flower buds of a bush native to the Mediterranean and parts of India. The buds are picked, sun-dried, then pickled. Capers should be rinsed before using to remove excess salt.

NUTRIENTS PER SERVING (3 snacks): Carbohydrate: 2 g, Fat: 5 g, Protein: 9 g, Calories: 83 (44% of calories from fat), Saturated Fat: 2 g, Sodium: 196 mg

Spicy Deviled Eggs

6 eggs
3 tablespoons heavy cream
1 green onion, finely chopped
1 tablespoon white wine vinegar
2 teaspoons Dijon mustard
½ teaspoon curry powder
½ teaspoon hot pepper sauce
3 tablespoons crisply cooked chopped bacon
1 tablespoon chopped fresh chives or parsley, for garnish

1. Place eggs in small saucepan; cover with cold water. Bring to a boil over high heat. Cover and remove from heat. Let stand 15 minutes. Drain; rinse under cold water. Peel eggs; cool completely.

2. Slice eggs in half lengthwise. Remove yolks to small bowl; set whites aside. Mash yolks with fork. Stir in cream, onion, vinegar, mustard, curry powder and pepper sauce until blended.

3. Spoon or pipe egg yolk mixture into centers of egg whites. Arrange eggs on serving plate. Sprinkle bacon over eggs. Garnish with chives, if desired.

Makes 12 deviled eggs

NUTRIENTS PER SERVING (2 deviled eggs): Carbohydrate: <1 g, Fat: 6 g, Protein: 6 g, Calories: 89 (67% of calories from fat), Saturated Fat: 2 g, Sodium: 85 mg

Angelic Deviled Eggs

6 eggs
¼ cup low-fat (1%) cottage cheese
3 tablespoons prepared fat-free ranch dressing
2 teaspoons Dijon mustard
2 tablespoons minced fresh chives or dill
1 tablespoon diced well-drained pimiento or roasted red pepper

1. Place eggs in medium saucepan; add enough water to cover. Bring to a boil over medium heat. Cover and remove from heat. Let stand 15 minutes. Drain; rinse under cool water. Peel eggs; cool completely.

2. Slice eggs lengthwise in half. Remove yolks, reserving 3 yolk halves. Discard remaining yolks or reserve for another use. Place egg whites, cut-sides up, on serving plate; cover with plastic wrap. Refrigerate while preparing filling.

3. Combine cottage cheese, dressing, mustard and reserved yolk halves in food processor; process until smooth. (Or, place in small bowl and mash with fork until well blended.) Transfer cheese mixture to small bowl; stir in chives and pimiento. Spoon into egg whites. Cover and chill at least 1 hour. Garnish, if desired.   *Makes 12 deviled eggs*

NUTRIENTS PER SERVING (1 deviled egg without garnish): Carbohydrate: 1 g, Fat: 1 g, Protein: 3 g, Calories: 24 (26% of calories from fat), Saturated Fat: <1 g, Sodium: 96 mg

Angelic Deviled Eggs

Jerk Wings with Ranch Dipping Sauce

½ cup mayonnaise
½ cup plain yogurt or sour cream
1½ teaspoons salt, divided
1¼ teaspoons garlic powder, divided
½ teaspoon black pepper, divided
¼ teaspoon onion powder
2 tablespoons orange juice
1 teaspoon sugar
1 teaspoon dried thyme leaves
1 teaspoon paprika
¼ teaspoon ground nutmeg
¼ teaspoon ground red pepper
2½ pounds chicken wings (about 10 wings)

1. Preheat oven to 450°F. For Ranch Dipping Sauce, combine mayonnaise, yogurt, ½ teaspoon salt, ¼ teaspoon garlic powder, ¼ teaspoon black pepper and onion powder in small bowl.

2. Combine orange juice, sugar, thyme, paprika, nutmeg, red pepper and remaining 1 teaspoon salt, 1 teaspoon garlic powder and ¼ teaspoon black pepper in small bowl.

3. Cut tips from wings; discard. Place wings in large bowl. Drizzle with orange juice mixture; toss to coat.

4. Transfer chicken to greased broiler pan. Bake 25 to 30 minutes or until juices run clear and skin is crisp. Serve with Ranch Dipping Sauce.   *Makes 6 to 7 servings*

Serving Suggestion: Serve with celery sticks, if desired.

NUTRIENTS PER SERVING (⅙ of total recipe): Carbohydrate: 4 g, Fat: 30 g, Protein: 20 g, Calories: 363 (50% of calories from fat), Saturated Fat: 12 g, Sodium: 699 mg

Jerk Wings with Ranch Dipping Sauce

Quick and Easy Stuffed Mushrooms

 1 slice whole wheat bread
16 large mushrooms
$\frac{1}{2}$ cup sliced celery
$\frac{1}{2}$ cup sliced onion
 1 clove garlic
   Nonstick cooking spray
 1 teaspoon Worcestershire sauce
$\frac{1}{2}$ teaspoon marjoram leaves, crushed
$\frac{1}{8}$ teaspoon ground red pepper
   Dash paprika

1. Tear bread into pieces; place in food processor. Process 30 seconds or until crumbs form. Transfer to small bowl; set aside.

2. Remove stems from mushrooms; reserve caps. Place mushroom stems, celery, onion and garlic in food processor. Process with on/off pulses until vegetables are finely chopped.

3. Preheat oven to 350°F. Coat nonstick skillet with cooking spray. Add vegetable mixture; cook and stir over medium heat 5 minutes or until onion is tender. Remove to bowl. Stir in bread crumbs, Worcestershire sauce, marjoram and ground red pepper.

4. Fill mushroom caps with mixture, pressing down firmly. Place filled caps in shallow baking pan about $\frac{1}{2}$ inch apart. Spray lightly with cooking spray. Sprinkle with paprika. Bake 15 minutes or until hot.   *Makes 8 servings*

Note: Mushrooms can be stuffed up to 1 day ahead. Refrigerate filled mushroom caps, covered, until ready to serve. Bake in preheated 300°F oven 20 minutes or until hot.

NUTRIENTS PER SERVING (2 stuffed mushrooms): Carbohydrate: 4 g, Fat: <1 g, Protein: 1 g, Calories: 20 (11% of calories from fat), Saturated Fat: <1 g, Sodium: 29 mg

Grilled Shrimp Over Greens

Prep Time: 10 minutes   *Marinate Time:* 1 hour   *Cook Time:* 5 minutes

¾ cup CARB OPTIONS™ Italian Dressing
1 pound uncooked medium shrimp, peeled and deveined
6 cups or 1 bag (10 ounces) mixed salad greens
¼ cup sliced radishes

1. In large, shallow nonaluminum baking dish, pour ¼ cup Carb Options Italian Dressing over shrimp; turn to coat. Cover; marinate in refrigerator, turning occasionally, up to 1 hour.

2. Remove shrimp from marinade, discarding marinade. Grill or broil shrimp, turning once and brushing with additional ¼ cup Dressing until shrimp turn pink.

3. To serve, toss remaining ¼ cup Dressing with greens and arrange on serving platter. Top with grilled shrimp and radishes.   *Makes 4 servings*

NUTRIENTS PER SERVING (¼ of total recipe): Carbohydrate: 2 g, Fat: 13 g, Protein: 20 g, Calories: 210 (56% of calories from fat), Saturated Fat: 2 g, Sodium: 730 mg

Cold Asparagus with Lemon-Mustard Dressing

12 fresh asparagus spears
2 tablespoons fat-free mayonnaise
1 tablespoon sweet brown mustard
1 tablespoon fresh lemon juice
1 teaspoon grated lemon peel, divided

1. Steam asparagus until crisp-tender and bright green; immediately drain and rinse under cold water. Cover and refrigerate until chilled.

2. Combine mayonnaise, mustard and lemon juice in small bowl; blend well. Stir in ½ teaspoon lemon peel; set aside.

3. Arrange asparagus on plate. Spoon dressing over asparagus. Sprinkle with lemon peel. Garnish as desired.   *Makes 2 appetizer servings*

NUTRIENTS PER SERVING (½ of total recipe): Carbohydrate: 7 g, Fat: 1 g, Protein: 3 g, Calories: 39 (14% of calories from fat), Saturated Fat: <1 g, Sodium: 294 mg

Cold Asparagus with Lemon-Mustard Dressing

Thai Lamb & Couscous Rolls

5 cups water, divided
16 large napa or Chinese cabbage leaves, stems trimmed
2 tablespoons minced fresh ginger
1 teaspoon red pepper flakes
²/₃ cup uncooked quick-cooking couscous
   Nonstick cooking spray
½ pound lean ground lamb
½ cup chopped green onions
3 cloves garlic, minced
¼ cup plus 2 tablespoons minced fresh cilantro or mint, divided
2 tablespoons reduced-sodium soy sauce
1 tablespoon lime juice
1 teaspoon dark sesame oil
1 cup plain nonfat yogurt

1. Place 4 cups water in medium saucepan; bring to a boil over high heat. Drop cabbage leaves into water; cook 30 seconds. Drain. Rinse under cold water until cool; pat dry.

2. Place 1 cup water, ginger and red pepper in medium saucepan; bring to a boil over high heat. Stir in couscous; cover. Remove saucepan from heat; let stand 5 minutes.

3. Spray large saucepan with cooking spray; add lamb, onions and garlic. Cook and stir over medium-high heat 5 minutes or until lamb is no longer pink; drain.

4. Combine couscous, lamb mixture, ¼ cup cilantro, soy sauce, lime juice and oil in medium bowl. Spoon evenly down centers of cabbage leaves. Fold ends of cabbage leaves over filling; roll up. Combine yogurt and remaining 2 tablespoons cilantro in small bowl; spoon evenly over rolls. Serve warm. Garnish, if desired.   *Makes 16 servings*

NUTRIENTS PER SERVING (1 roll with 1 tablespoon yogurt sauce):
Carbohydrate: 7 g, Fat: 1 g, Protein: 4 g, Calories: 53 (16% of calories from fat), Saturated Fat: <1 g, Sodium: 75 mg

Thai Lamb & Couscous Rolls

Hot Artichoke Dip

Prep Time: 5 minutes   *Cook Time:* 25 minutes

1 can (14 ounces) artichoke hearts, drained and chopped
1 cup CARB OPTIONS™ Whipped Dressing
1 cup grated Parmesan cheese (about 4 ounces)
1 clove garlic, finely chopped *or* ¼ teaspoon LAWRY'S® Garlic Powder With
**   Parsley (optional)**

1. Preheat oven to 350°F.

2. In 1-quart casserole, combine all ingredients. Bake uncovered 25 minutes or until heated through. Serve with your favorite dippers.   *Makes 40 servings*

NUTRIENTS PER SERVING (1 tablespoon): Carbohydrate: 1 g, Fat: 3 g, Protein: 1 g, Calories: 35 (77% of calories from fat), Saturated Fat: 1 g, Sodium: 110 mg

Red Hot Pepper Wings

28 chicken wing drumettes (2¼ to 3 pounds)
 2 tablespoons olive oil
   Salt and black pepper
 2 tablespoons melted butter
 1 teaspoon sugar
¼ to ½ cup hot pepper sauce

Brush chicken with oil; sprinkle with salt and pepper. Grill chicken on covered grill over medium KINGSFORD® Briquets about 20 minutes until juices run clear, turning every 5 minutes. Combine butter, sugar and pepper sauce in large bowl; add chicken and toss to coat. Serve hot or cold.   *Makes 7 servings*

NUTRIENTS PER SERVING (4 drumettes): Carbohydrate: 4 g, Fat: 39 g, Protein: 36 g, Calories: 503 (70% of calories from fat), Saturated Fat: 11 g, Sodium: 222 mg

Quick Pickled Green Beans

½ pound (3½ cups loosely packed) whole green beans
½ red bell pepper, cut into strips (optional)
1 jalapeño* or other hot pepper, cut into strips
1 large clove garlic, cut in half
1 bay leaf
1 cup white wine vinegar
1 cup water
½ cup white wine
1 tablespoon sugar
1 tablespoon salt
1 tablespoon whole coriander seeds
1 tablespoon mustard seeds
1 tablespoon whole peppercorns

Jalapeño peppers can sting and irritate the skin; wear rubber gloves when handling peppers and do not touch eyes. Wash hands after handling.

1. Wash green beans and remove stem ends. Place in a glass dish just large enough to hold green beans and 2½ cups liquid. Add bell pepper strips, if desired. Tuck jalapeño strips, garlic and bay leaf between beans.

2. Place remaining ingredients in medium saucepan. Bring to a boil, stirring to dissolve sugar and salt. Reduce heat and simmer 5 minutes. Pour mixture over green beans. They should be submerged in liquid. If not, add additional hot water to cover.

3. Cover and refrigerate at least 24 hours. Remove and discard bay leaf before serving. Flavor improves in 48 hours and beans may be kept refrigerated for up to five days. Remove green beans from liquid before serving. *Makes 6 appetizer servings*

NUTRIENTS PER SERVING (⅙ of total recipe): Carbohydrate: 4 g, Fat: <1 g, Protein: 1 g, Calories: 21 (6% of calories from fat), Saturated Fat: <1 g, Sodium: 119 mg

Chicken Satay

Prep and Cook Time: 30 minutes

1 pound chicken tenders or boneless skinless chicken breasts, cut into 8 strips
2 tablespoons light soy sauce

Satay Dipping Sauce
Nonstick cooking spray
2 tablespoons finely chopped onion
1 clove garlic, minced
Dash ground ginger
½ cup regular or reduced-fat chunky peanut butter
3 to 4 tablespoons light soy sauce
3 to 4 tablespoons white wine vinegar or rice wine vinegar
1 teaspoon sugar

1. Place chicken in 8×8-inch baking pan; drizzle with 2 tablespoons soy sauce and toss. Let stand 5 to 10 minutes.

2. Thread 1 chicken tender on metal or bamboo* skewer. Repeat with remaining chicken tenders. Arrange skewers on broiler pan. Broil 4 inches from heat 3 to 5 minutes per side or until chicken is no longer pink in center.

3. Meanwhile, prepare Satay Dipping Sauce. Spray small saucepan with cooking spray; heat over medium heat until hot. Add onion, garlic and ginger; cook and stir 2 to 3 minutes or until onion is tender. Add remaining ingredients; cook 5 minutes, stirring constantly, until smooth and hot. Spoon into bowl for dipping; serve with chicken.

Makes 8 servings

Soak bamboo skewers in water 20 minutes before using to prevent burning.

NUTRIENTS PER SERVING (1 chicken tender with about 2 tablespoons dipping sauce): Carbohydrate: 5 g, Fat: 9 g, Protein: 17 g, Calories: 171 (47% of calories from fat), Saturated Fat: 2 g, Sodium: 372 mg

Chicken Satay

Mexican Roll-Ups

6 uncooked lasagna noodles
¾ cup prepared guacamole
¾ cup chunky salsa
¾ cup (3 ounces) shredded fat-free Cheddar cheese
Additional salsa (optional)

1. Cook lasagna noodles according to package directions, omitting salt. Rinse with cool water; drain. Pat dry; cool.

2. Spread 2 tablespoons guacamole onto each noodle; top each with 2 tablespoons salsa and 2 tablespoons cheese.

3. Roll up noodles jelly-roll fashion. Cut each roll-up in half to form two equal-size roll-ups. Serve immediately with additional salsa, if desired, or cover with plastic wrap and refrigerate up to 3 hours.   *Makes 12 appetizers*

NUTRIENTS PER SERVING (1 roll-up): Carbohydrate: 4 g, Fat: 1 g, Protein: 3 g, Calories: 40 (28% of calories from fat), Saturated Fat: 0 g, Sodium: 218 mg

Turkey-Broccoli Roll-Ups

2 pounds broccoli spears
⅓ cup fat-free sour cream
¼ cup reduced-fat mayonnaise
2 tablespoons thawed frozen orange juice concentrate
1 tablespoon Dijon mustard
1 teaspoon dried basil leaves
1 pound smoked turkey, very thinly sliced

1. Arrange broccoli spears in single layer in large, shallow microwavable dish. Add 1 tablespoon water. Cover dish tightly with plastic wrap; vent. Microwave at HIGH 6 to 7 minutes or just until broccoli is crisp-tender, rearranging spears after 4 minutes. Carefully remove plastic wrap; drain broccoli. Immediately place broccoli in cold water to stop cooking; drain well. Pat dry with paper towels.

2. Combine sour cream, mayonnaise, juice concentrate, mustard and basil in small bowl.

3. Cut turkey slices into 2-inch-wide strips. Spread sour cream mixture evenly on strips. Place 1 broccoli piece at short end of each strip. Starting at short end, roll up tightly (allow broccoli spear to protrude from one end). Place on serving platter; cover with plastic wrap. Refrigerate until ready to serve. Garnish just before serving, if desired.

Makes 20 servings

Note: To blanch broccoli on stove top, bring small amount of water to a boil in saucepan. Add broccoli spears; cover. Simmer 2 to 3 minutes or until broccoli is crisp-tender; drain. Continue as directed.

NUTRIENTS PER SERVING (2 roll-ups): Carbohydrate: 4 g, Fat: 1 g, Protein: 7 g, Calories: 51 (19% of calories from fat), Saturated Fat: <1 g, Sodium: 259 mg

Turkey-Broccoli Roll-Ups

Broiled SPAM™ Appetizers

1 (7-ounce) can SPAM® Classic, finely cubed
⅓ cup shredded Cheddar cheese
¼ cup finely chopped celery
¼ cup mayonnaise or salad dressing
1 tablespoon chopped fresh parsley
⅛ teaspoon hot pepper sauce
   Toast triangles, party rye slices or crackers

In medium bowl, combine all ingredients except toast. Spread mixture on toast triangles. Place on baking sheet. Broil 1 to 2 minutes or until cheese is melted.

Makes 32 appetizers

NUTRIENTS PER SERVING (1 appetizer without toast): Carbohydrate: <1 g, Fat: 4 g, Protein: 1 g, Calories: 39 (87% of calories from fat), Saturated Fat: 1 g, Sodium: 100 mg

Fast Guacamole and "Chips"

2 ripe avocados
½ cup restaurant-style chunky salsa
¼ teaspoon hot pepper sauce (optional)
½ seedless cucumber, sliced into ⅛-inch rounds

1. Cut avocados in half; remove and discard pits. Scoop flesh into medium bowl. Mash with fork.

2. Add salsa and pepper sauce, if desired; mix well.

3. Transfer guacamole to serving bowl; surround with cucumber "chips".

Makes 8 servings (about 1¾ cups)

NUTRIENTS PER SERVING (about 3½ tablespoons guacamole plus cucumbers): Carbohydrate: 5 g, Fat: 7 g, Protein: 2 g, Calories: 85 (72% of calories from fat), Saturated Fat: 1 g, Sodium: 120 mg

Spicy Chicken Wings with Ranch Dressing

Prep Time: 10 minutes   *Cook Time:* 1 hour

   24 chicken wings (about 2 pounds)
   ²⁄₃ cup cayenne pepper sauce
   ¹⁄₃ cup I CAN'T BELIEVE IT'S NOT BUTTER!® Spread
1¹⁄₂ teaspoons cayenne pepper*
   CARB OPTIONS™ Ranch Dressing

Use more or less as desired.

1. Preheat oven to 425°F.

2. Cut tips off wings; cut wings in half at joint. In bowl, combine cayenne pepper sauce, Spread and pepper. Stir in wings until coated.

3. In roasting pan or bottom of broiler pan, arrange wings. Bake 1 hour or until wings are thoroughly cooked and crisp. Serve with Carb Options Ranch Dressing.

Makes 12 servings

NUTRIENTS PER SERVING (¹⁄₂ cup): Carbohydrate: 1 g, Fat: 27 g, Protein: 11 g, Calories: 290 (84% of calories from fat), Saturated Fat: 5 g, Sodium: 45 mg

Seize the Day

Southwest Ham 'n Cheese Quiche

    4 (8-inch) flour tortillas
    2 tablespoons butter or margarine, melted
    2 cups pizza 4-cheese blend
 1½ cups (8 ounces) diced CURE 81® ham
    ½ cup sour cream
    ¼ cup salsa
    3 eggs, beaten
       Salsa
       Sour cream

Heat oven to 350°F. Cut 3 tortillas in half. Place remaining whole tortilla in bottom of greased 10-inch quiche dish or tart pan; brush with melted butter. Arrange tortilla halves around edge of dish, rounded sides up, overlapping to form pastry shell. Brush with remaining butter. Place 9-inch round cake pan inside quiche dish. Bake 5 minutes. Cool; remove cake pan. In large bowl, combine cheese and ham. Stir in sour cream, salsa and eggs. Pour into tortilla shell. Bake 55 to 60 minutes or until knife inserted in center comes out clean. Let stand 5 minutes. Serve with additional salsa and sour cream.

Makes 6 servings

NUTRIENTS PER SERVING (⅙ of total recipe): Carbohydrate: 15 g, Fat: 21 g, Protein: 23 g, Calories: 332 (57% of calories from fat), Saturated Fat: 9 g, Sodium: 762 mg

Easy Brunch Frittata

Nonstick cooking spray
1 cup small broccoli florets
2½ cups (12 ounces) frozen hash brown potatoes with onions
   and peppers (O'Brien style), thawed
1½ cups cholesterol-free egg substitute
2 tablespoons reduced-fat (2%) milk
¾ teaspoon salt
¼ teaspoon black pepper
½ cup (2 ounces) shredded reduced-fat Cheddar cheese
Sour cream (optional)

1. Preheat oven to 450°F. Coat medium nonstick ovenproof skillet with cooking spray. Heat skillet over medium heat until hot. Add broccoli; cook and stir 2 minutes. Add potatoes; cook and stir 5 minutes.

2. Beat together egg substitute, milk, salt and pepper in small bowl; pour over potato mixture. Cook 5 minutes or until edge is set (center will still be wet).

3. Transfer skillet to oven; bake 6 minutes or until center is set. Remove from oven. Sprinkle with cheese; let stand 2 to 3 minutes or until cheese is melted.

4. Cut into wedges; serve with sour cream, if desired.   *Makes 6 servings*

NUTRIENTS PER SERVING (1 frittata wedge without sour cream):
Carbohydrate: 11 g, Fat: 2 g, Protein: 9 g, Calories: 102 (20% of calories from fat), Saturated Fat: 1 g, Sodium: 627 mg

Easy Brunch Frittata

Western Omelet

Prep Time: 15 minutes   *Cook Time:* 10 minutes

- ½ **cup finely chopped red or green bell pepper**
- ⅓ **cup cubed cooked potato**
- 2 **slices turkey bacon, diced**
- ¼ **teaspoon dried oregano leaves**
- 2 **teaspoons FLEISCHMANN'S® Original Margarine, divided**
- 1 **cup EGG BEATERS®**
- **Fresh oregano sprig, for garnish**

In 8-inch nonstick skillet, over medium heat, sauté bell pepper, potato, turkey bacon and dried oregano in 1 teaspoon margarine until tender. Remove from skillet; keep warm.

In same skillet, over medium heat, melt remaining margarine. Pour Egg Beaters® into skillet. Cook, lifting edges to allow uncooked portion to flow underneath. When almost set, spoon vegetable mixture over half of omelet. Fold other half over vegetable mixture; slide onto serving plate. Garnish with fresh oregano.   *Makes 2 servings*

Western Frittata: Sauté vegetables, turkey bacon and dried oregano in 2 teaspoons margarine. Pour Egg Beaters® evenly into skillet over vegetable mixture. Cook without stirring for 4 to 5 minutes or until cooked on bottom and almost set on top. Carefully turn frittata; cook for 1 to 2 minutes more or until done. Slide onto serving platter; cut into wedges to serve.

NUTRIENTS PER SERVING (½ of omelet): Carbohydrate: 14 g, Fat: 6 g, Protein: 15 g, Calories: 166 (30% of calories from fat), Saturated Fat: 1 g, Sodium: 423 mg

Western Omelet

Deep South Ham and Redeye Gravy

1 tablespoon butter
1 ham steak (about 1⅓ pounds)
1 cup strong coffee
¾ teaspoon sugar
¼ teaspoon hot pepper sauce

1. Heat large skillet over medium-high heat until hot. Add butter; tilt skillet to coat bottom. Add ham steak; cook 3 minutes. Turn; cook 2 minutes longer or until lightly browned. Remove ham to serving platter; set aside and keep warm.

2. Add coffee, sugar and pepper sauce to same skillet. Bring to a boil over high heat; boil 2 to 3 minutes or until liquid is reduced to ¼ cup, scraping up any brown bits. Serve gravy over ham. *Makes 4 servings*

Serving Suggestion: Serve ham steak with sautéed greens and poached eggs.

NUTRIENTS PER SERVING (¼ of total recipe): Carbohydrate: 1 g, Fat: 9 g, Protein: 30 g, Calories: 215 (38% of calories from fat), Saturated Fat: 1 g, Sodium: 2 mg

Deep South Ham and Redeye Gravy

Cinnamon Flats

1¾ cups all-purpose flour
½ cup sugar
1½ teaspoons ground cinnamon
¼ teaspoon ground nutmeg
¼ teaspoon salt
8 tablespoons cold margarine
3 egg whites, divided
1 teaspoon vanilla
1 teaspoon water
   Sugar Glaze (page 54)

1. Preheat oven to 350°F. Combine flour, sugar, cinnamon, nutmeg and salt in medium bowl. Cut in margarine with pastry blender or two knives until mixture forms coarse crumbs. Beat in 2 egg whites and vanilla, forming crumbly mixture; mix with hands to form soft dough.

2. Divide dough into 6 equal pieces and place, evenly spaced, on greased 15×10-inch jelly-roll pan. Spread dough evenly to edges of pan using hands; smooth top of dough with metal spatula or palms of hands. Mix remaining egg white and water in small cup; brush over top of dough. Lightly score dough into 2×1½-inch squares.

3. Bake 20 to 25 minutes or until lightly browned and firm. While still warm, cut into squares along score lines; drizzle or spread Sugar Glaze over squares. Let stand 15 minutes or until glaze is firm before removing from pan.

Makes 50 cookies

NUTRIENTS PER SERVING (1 cookie): Carbohydrate: 9 g, Fat: 1 g, Protein: 1 g, Calories: 48 (18% of calories from fat), Saturated Fat: <1 g, Sodium: 35 mg

continued on page 54

Cinnamon Flats, continued

Sugar Glaze

1¹/₂ **cups powdered sugar**
  2 to 3 tablespoons fat-free (skim) milk
  1 teaspoon vanilla

Combine powdered sugar, 2 tablespoons milk and vanilla in small bowl. If glaze is too thick, add remaining 1 tablespoon milk. *Makes about ³/₄ cup*

Mushroom-Herb Omelet

Prep Time: 10 minutes   *Cook Time:* 20 minutes

  1 cup EGG BEATERS®
  1 tablespoon chopped fresh parsley
  1 teaspoon finely chopped oregano, basil or thyme (*or* ¹/₄ teaspoon dried)
  2 cups sliced fresh mushrooms
  2 teaspoons FLEISCHMANN'S® Original Margarine, divided

In small bowl, combine Egg Beaters®, parsley and oregano, basil or thyme; set aside.

In 8-inch nonstick skillet, over medium heat, sauté mushrooms in 1 teaspoon margarine until tender; set aside. In same skillet, over medium heat, melt ¹/₂ teaspoon margarine. Pour half the egg mixture into skillet. Cook, lifting edge to allow uncooked portion to flow underneath. When almost set, spoon half of mushrooms over half of omelet. Fold other half over mushrooms; slide onto serving plate. Repeat with remaining margarine, egg mixture and mushrooms. *Makes 2 servings*

NUTRIENTS PER SERVING (1 omelet): Carbohydrate: 7 g, Fat: 3 g, Protein: 14 g, Calories: 114 (27% of calories from fat), Saturated Fat: 1 g, Sodium: 239 mg

Spinach Sensation

½ **pound bacon slices**
1 **cup (8 ounces) sour cream**
3 **eggs, separated**
2 **tablespoons all-purpose flour**
⅛ **teaspoon black pepper**
1 **package (10 ounces) frozen chopped spinach, thawed and squeezed dry**
½ **cup (2 ounces) shredded sharp Cheddar cheese**
½ **cup dry bread crumbs**
1 **tablespoon margarine or butter, melted**

1. Preheat oven to 350°F. Spray 2-quart round baking dish with nonstick cooking spray.

2. Place bacon in single layer in large skillet; cook over medium heat until crisp. Remove from skillet; drain on paper towels. Crumble and set aside.

3. Combine sour cream, egg yolks, flour and pepper in large bowl; set aside. Beat egg whites in medium bowl at high speed of electric mixer until stiff peaks form. Stir ¼ of egg whites into sour cream mixture; fold in remaining egg whites.

4. Arrange ½ of spinach in prepared dish. Top with ½ of sour cream mixture. Sprinkle ¼ cup cheese over sour cream mixture. Sprinkle bacon over cheese. Repeat layers, ending with remaining ¼ cup cheese.

5. Combine bread crumbs and margarine in small bowl; sprinkle evenly over cheese. Bake, uncovered, 30 to 35 minutes or until egg mixture is set. Let stand 5 minutes before serving.   *Makes 6 servings*

NUTRIENTS PER SERVING (⅙ of total recipe): Carbohydrate: 12 g, Fat: 23 g, Protein: 14 g, Calories: 335 (67% of calories from fat), Saturated Fat: 11 g, Sodium: 547 mg

Chile Cheese Puff

¾ **cup all-purpose flour**
1½ **teaspoons baking powder**
9 **eggs**
4 **cups (16 ounces) shredded Monterey Jack cheese**
2 **cups (16 ounces) 1% low-fat cottage cheese**
2 **cans (4 ounces each) diced green chilies, drained**
1½ **teaspoons sugar**
¼ **teaspoon salt**
⅛ **teaspoon hot pepper sauce**
1 **cup salsa**

1. Preheat oven to 350°F. Spray 13×9-inch baking dish with nonstick cooking spray.

2. Combine flour and baking powder in small bowl.

3. Whisk eggs in large bowl until blended; stir in Monterey Jack, cottage cheese, chilies, sugar, salt and hot pepper sauce. Add flour mixture; stir just until combined. Pour into prepared dish.

4. Bake, uncovered, 45 minutes or until set. Let stand 5 minutes before serving. Serve with salsa.   *Makes 8 servings*

NUTRIENTS PER SERVING (⅛ of total recipe): Carbohydrate: 14 g, Fat: 23 g, Protein: 29 g, Calories: 393 (53% of calories from fat), Saturated Fat: <1 g, Sodium: 1060 mg

Chile Cheese Puff

Zucchini-Tomato Frittata

Nonstick olive oil cooking spray
1 cup sliced zucchini
1 cup broccoli florets
1 cup diced red or yellow bell pepper
3 whole eggs, lightly beaten*
5 egg whites, lightly beaten*
½ cup 1% low-fat cottage cheese
½ cup rehydrated sun-dried tomatoes (1 ounce dry), coarsely chopped
¼ cup chopped green onions with tops
¼ cup chopped fresh basil
⅛ teaspoon ground red pepper
2 tablespoons Parmesan cheese
Paprika (optional)

Or, substitute 1½ cups cholesterol-free egg substitute.

1. Preheat broiler. Spray 10-inch ovenproof nonstick skillet with cooking spray. Place zucchini, broccoli and bell pepper in skillet; cook and stir over high heat 3 to 4 minutes or until crisp-tender.

2. Combine whole eggs, egg whites, cottage cheese, tomatoes, onions, basil and ground red pepper in medium bowl; mix well. Pour egg mixture over vegetables in skillet. Cook uncovered, gently lifting sides of frittata so uncooked egg flows underneath. Cook 7 to 8 minutes or until frittata is almost firm and golden brown on bottom. Remove from heat. Sprinkle with Parmesan.

3. Broil about 5 inches from heat 3 to 5 minutes or until golden brown. Garnish with paprika, if desired. Cut into 4 wedges. Serve immediately.   *Makes 4 servings*

NUTRIENTS PER SERVING (1 frittata wedge): Carbohydrate: 13 g, Fat: 5 g, Protein: 16 g, Calories: 160 (29% of calories from fat), Saturated Fat: 2 g, Sodium: 305 mg

Zucchini-Tomato Frittata

Mini Vegetable Quiches

2 cups cut-up vegetables (bell peppers, broccoli, zucchini and/or carrots)
2 tablespoons chopped green onions
2 tablespoons FLEISCHMANN'S® Original Margarine
4 (8-inch) flour tortillas, each cut into 8 triangles
1 cup EGG BEATERS®
1 cup fat-free (skim) milk
½ teaspoon dried basil leaves

In medium nonstick skillet, over medium-high heat, sauté vegetables and green onions in margarine until tender.

Arrange 4 tortilla triangles in each of 8 (6-ounce) greased custard cups or ramekins, placing points of tortillas at center of bottom of each cup and pressing lightly to form shape of cup. Divide vegetable mixture evenly among cups. In small bowl, combine Egg Beaters®, milk and basil. Pour evenly over vegetable mixture. Place cups on baking sheet. Bake at 375°F for 20 to 25 minutes or until puffed and knife inserted into centers comes out clean. Let stand 5 minutes before serving.   *Makes 8 servings*

NUTRIENTS PER SERVING (1 mini quiche): Carbohydrate: 14 g, Fat: 4 g, Protein: 6 g, Calories: 115 (30% of calories from fat), Saturated Fat: 1 g, Sodium: 184 mg

Mini Vegetable Quiches

Apple and Brie Omelet

2 large Golden Delicious apples
2 tablespoons butter or margarine, divided
½ teaspoon ground nutmeg
4 ounces Brie cheese
8 large eggs, lightly beaten
2 green onions, thinly sliced

1. Place large serving platter in oven and preheat to 200°F. Peel, core and slice apples; place in microwavable container. Top with 1 tablespoon butter and nutmeg. Cover and microwave at HIGH 3 minutes. Set aside. While apples cook, trim rind from cheese; thinly slice cheese.

2. Whisk eggs in medium bowl until blended. Melt 1½ teaspoons butter in medium nonstick skillet over medium heat; rotate skillet to coat bottom. Pour half of eggs into skillet. Cook without stirring 1 to 2 minutes or until set on bottom. Lift side of omelet and slightly tilt pan to allow uncooked portion of egg to flow underneath. Cover pan and cook 2 to 3 minutes or until eggs are set but still moist on top. Remove platter from oven and slide omelet into center. Spread apples evenly over entire omelet, reserving a few slices for garnish, if desired. Evenly space cheese slices over apples. Sprinkle with onion, reserving some for garnish. Return platter to oven.

3. Cook remaining beaten eggs in remaining 1½ teaspoons butter as directed above. When cooked, slide spatula around edge to be certain omelet is loose. Carefully place second omelet over cheese, apple and onion mixture. Top with reserved apple and onion slices. Cut into wedges to serve.

Makes 4 servings

NUTRIENTS PER SERVING (1 omelet wedge): Carbohydrate: 11 g, Fat: 24 g, Protein: 19 g, Calories: 334 (64% of calories from fat), Saturated Fat: 11 g, Sodium: 362 mg

Apple and Brie Omelet

Baked Eggs Florentine

Prep and Cook Time: 28 minutes

2 packages (10 ounces each) frozen creamed spinach
4 slices (⅛ inch thick) deli ham, about 5 to 6 ounces
4 eggs
   Salt and black pepper
⅛ teaspoon ground nutmeg
½ cup (2 ounces) shredded provolone cheese
2 tablespoons chopped roasted red pepper

1. Preheat oven to 450°F. Make small cut in each package of spinach. Microwave at HIGH 5 to 6 minutes, turning packages halfway through cooking time.

2. Meanwhile, grease 8-inch square baking pan. Place ham slices on bottom of prepared pan, overlapping slightly. Spread spinach over ham slices.

3. Make 4 indentations in spinach. Carefully break 1 egg in each. Season with salt and black pepper. Sprinkle with nutmeg.

4. Bake 16 to 19 minutes or until eggs are set. Remove from oven. Sprinkle cheese and red pepper over top. Return to oven and bake 1 to 2 minutes longer or until cheese is melted. Serve immediately.
Makes 4 servings

NUTRIENTS PER SERVING (¼ of total recipe): Carbohydrate: 15 g, Fat: 14 g, Protein: 21 g, Calories: 254 (50% of calories from fat), Saturated Fat: 7 g, Sodium: 1163 mg

Baked Eggs Florentine

Chile Scramble

Prep Time: 5 minutes   *Cook Time:* 10 minutes

2 tablespoons minced onion
1 teaspoon FLEISCHMANN'S® Original Margarine
1 cup EGG BEATERS®
1 (4-ounce) can diced green chiles, drained
¼ cup whole kernel corn
2 tablespoons diced pimientos

In 10-inch nonstick skillet, over medium-high heat, sauté onion in margarine for 2 to 3 minutes or until onion is translucent. Pour Egg Beaters® into skillet; cook, stirring occasionally, until mixture is set. Stir in chiles, corn and pimientos; cook 1 minute more or until heated through.   *Makes 2 servings*

NUTRIENTS PER SERVING (½ of total recipe): Carbohydrate: 13 g, Fat: 2 g, Protein: 13 g, Calories: 122 (12% of calories from fat), Saturated Fat: <1 g, Sodium: 427 mg

Chile Scramble

Roasted Pepper and Sourdough Brunch Casserole

3 cups sourdough bread cubes
1 jar (12 ounces) roasted pepper strips, drained
1 cup (4 ounces) shredded reduced-fat sharp Cheddar cheese
1 cup (4 ounces) shredded reduced-fat Monterey Jack cheese
1 cup fat-free cottage cheese
1½ cups (12 ounces) cholesterol-free egg substitute
1 cup fat-free (skim) milk
¼ cup chopped fresh cilantro
¼ teaspoon black pepper

1. Spray 11×7-inch baking dish with nonstick cooking spray. Place bread cubes in dish. Arrange roasted peppers evenly over bread cubes. Sprinkle Cheddar and Monterey Jack cheeses over peppers.

2. Place cottage cheese in food processor or blender; process until smooth. Add egg substitute; process 10 seconds. Combine cottage cheese mixture and milk in small bowl; pour over ingredients in baking dish. Sprinkle with cilantro and black pepper. Cover with plastic wrap; refrigerate 4 to 12 hours.

3. Preheat oven to 375°F. Bake, uncovered, 40 minutes or until hot and bubbly and golden brown on top. *Makes 8 servings*

NUTRIENTS PER SERVING (about ¾ cup casserole): Carbohydrate: 13 g, Fat: 6 g, Protein: 19 g, Calories: 179 (28% of calories from fat), Saturated Fat: 3 g, Sodium: 704 mg

Spinach-Cheddar Squares

Prep Time: 15 minutes   *Cook Time:* 40 minutes

1 ½ cups **EGG BEATERS**®
¾ **cup fat-free (skim) milk**
1 **tablespoon dried onion flakes**
1 **tablespoon grated Parmesan cheese**
¼ **teaspoon garlic powder**
⅛ **teaspoon ground black pepper**
¼ **cup plain dry bread crumbs**
¾ **cup shredded fat-free Cheddar cheese, divided**
1 **(10-ounce) package frozen chopped spinach, thawed and well drained**
¼ **cup diced pimentos**

In medium bowl, combine Egg Beaters®, milk, onion flakes, Parmesan cheese, garlic powder and pepper; set aside.

Sprinkle bread crumbs evenly onto bottom of lightly greased 8×8×2-inch baking dish. Top with ½ cup Cheddar cheese and spinach. Pour egg mixture evenly over spinach; top with remaining Cheddar cheese and pimentos.

Bake at 350°F for 35 to 40 minutes or until knife inserted into center comes out clean. Let stand 10 minutes before serving.   *Makes 16 squares*

NUTRIENTS PER SERVING (1 square): Carbohydrate: 4 g, Fat: <1 g, Protein: 5 g, Calories: 37 (6% of calories from fat), Saturated Fat: <1 g, Sodium: 116 mg

Warming Up

Chunky Chicken and Vegetable Soup

1 tablespoon canola oil
1 boneless skinless chicken breast (4 ounces), diced
½ cup chopped green bell pepper
½ cup thinly sliced celery
2 green onions, sliced
2 cans (14½ ounces each) chicken broth
1 cup water
½ cup sliced carrots
2 tablespoons cream
1 tablespoon finely chopped parsley
¼ teaspoon dried thyme leaves
⅛ teaspoon black pepper

1. Heat oil in large saucepan over medium heat. Add chicken; cook and stir 4 to 5 minutes or until no longer pink. Add bell pepper, celery and onions. Cook and stir 7 minutes or until vegetables are tender.

2. Add broth, water, carrots, cream, parsley, thyme and black pepper. Simmer 10 minutes or until carrots are tender. *Makes 4 servings*

NUTRIENTS PER SERVING (¼ of total recipe): Carbohydrate: 5 g, Fat: 8 g, Protein: 9 g, Calories: 130 (57% of calories from fat), Saturated Fat: 3 g, Sodium: 895 mg

Italian Sausage and Vegetable Stew

Prep and Cook Time: 30 minutes

1 pound hot or mild Italian sausage links, cut into 1-inch pieces
1 package (16 ounces) frozen vegetable blend, such as onions and green, red and yellow bell peppers
2 medium zucchini, sliced
1 can (14½ ounces) diced Italian-style tomatoes, undrained
1 jar (4½ ounces) sliced mushrooms, drained
4 cloves garlic, minced

1. Cook sausage in large saucepan, covered, over medium to medium-high heat 5 minutes or until browned; pour off drippings.

2. Add frozen vegetables, zucchini, tomatoes with juice, mushrooms and garlic; bring to a boil. Reduce heat and simmer, covered, 10 minutes. Cook uncovered 5 to 10 minutes or until thickened slightly.   *Makes 6 servings*

NUTRIENTS PER SERVING (1 cup stew): Carbohydrate: 15 g, Fat: 22 g, Protein: 20 g, Calories: 340 (57% of calories from fat), Saturated Fat: 10 g, Sodium: 1110 mg

Italian Sausage and Vegetable Stew

Pepperoni Pizza Soup

1 tablespoon oil
1 cup sliced mushrooms
1 cup chopped green bell pepper
½ cup chopped onion
1 can (15 ounces) pizza sauce
1 can (14½ ounces) chicken broth
1 cup water
3 ounces sliced pepperoni
1 teaspoon dried oregano leaves
1 cup (4 ounces) shredded mozzarella cheese

1. Heat oil in large saucepan over medium heat. Add mushrooms, bell pepper and onion. Cook, stirring frequently, 7 minutes or until vegetables are tender.

2. Stir in pizza sauce, broth, water, pepperoni and oregano. Bring to a boil. Reduce heat and simmer 5 minutes. Serve with cheese.   *Makes 4 servings*

Tip: People following low-carb meal plans often say they miss pizza more than any other food. This recipe satisfies that craving with great pizza flavor and a minimum carbohydrate count!

NUTRIENTS PER SERVING (¼ of total recipe): Carbohydrate: 16 g, Fat: 18 g, Protein: 15 g, Calories: 287 (56% of calories from fat), Saturated Fat: 7 g, Sodium: 1566 mg

Pepperoni Pizza Soup

Pozole

Prep and Cook Time: 20 minutes

    1 large onion, thinly sliced
    1 tablespoon olive oil
    2 teaspoons dried oregano leaves
    1 clove garlic, minced
   ½ teaspoon ground cumin
    2 cans (14½ ounces each) chicken broth
    1 package (10 ounces) frozen corn
    1 to 2 cans (4 ounces each) chopped green chilies, undrained
    1 can (2¼ ounces) sliced ripe olives, drained
   ¾ pound boneless skinless chicken breasts
    Chopped fresh cilantro, for garnish

1. Combine onion, oil, oregano, garlic and cumin in Dutch oven. Cover and cook over medium heat about 6 minutes or until onion is tender, stirring occasionally.

2. Stir broth, corn, chilies and olives into onion mixture. Cover and bring to a boil over high heat.

3. While soup is cooking, cut chicken into thin strips. Add to soup. Reduce heat to medium-low; cover and cook 3 to 4 minutes or until chicken is no longer pink. Garnish with cilantro, if desired.
Makes 6 servings

NUTRIENTS PER SERVING (⅙ of total recipe): Carbohydrate: 14 g, Fat: 5 g, Protein: 16 g, Calories: 156 (27% of calories from fat), Saturated Fat: <1 g, Sodium: 739 mg

Pozole

Pasta Meatball Soup

10 ounces 95% ground beef sirloin
5 tablespoons acini di pepe pasta*, divided
¼ cup fresh fine bread crumbs
1 egg
2 tablespoons finely chopped fresh parsley, divided
1 teaspoon dried basil leaves, divided
¼ teaspoon salt
⅛ teaspoon black pepper
1 clove garlic, minced
2 cans (14½ ounces each) fat-free reduced-sodium beef broth
1 can (8 ounces) tomato sauce
⅓ cup chopped onion

*Acini di pepe is tiny rice-shaped pasta. Orzo or pastina can be substituted.

1. Combine beef, 2 tablespoons pasta, bread crumbs, egg, 1 tablespoon parsley, ½ teaspoon basil, salt, pepper and garlic in medium bowl. Shape into 28 to 30 (1-inch) meatballs.

2. Bring broth, tomato sauce, onion and remaining ½ teaspoon basil to a boil in large saucepan over medium-high heat. Carefully add meatballs to broth. Reduce heat to medium-low; simmer, covered, 20 minutes. Add remaining 3 tablespoons pasta; cook 10 minutes or until tender. Garnish with remaining 1 tablespoon parsley.

Makes 4 servings

NUTRIENTS PER SERVING (1½ cups): Carbohydrate: 15 g, Fat: 7 g, Protein: 22 g, Calories: 216 (30% of calories from fat), Saturated Fat: 2 g, Sodium: 599 mg

Pasta Meatball Soup

Main Dish Chicken Soup

1 can (49½ ounces) fat-free, reduced-sodium chicken broth *or* 3 cans (14½ ounces each) fat-free, reduced-sodium chicken broth plus 6 ounces of water
1 cup grated carrots
½ cup sliced green onions
½ cup diced red bell pepper
½ cup frozen green peas
1 seedless cucumber
12 chicken tenders (about 1 pound)
½ teaspoon white pepper

1. Bring broth to a boil in large 4-quart Dutch oven over high heat. Add carrots, green onions, red pepper and peas. Return to a boil. Reduce heat and simmer 3 minutes.

2. Meanwhile, cut ends off cucumber and discard. Using vegetable peeler, start at top and make long, noodle-like strips of cucumber. Slice any remaining cucumber pieces thinly with knife. Add cucumber strips to Dutch oven; simmer until cucumber strips are cooked.

3. Add chicken tenders and white pepper; simmer 5 minutes or until chicken is no longer pink.   *Makes 6 servings*

NUTRIENTS PER SERVING (⅙ of total recipe): Carbohydrate: 7 g, Fat: 3 g, Protein: 26 g, Calories: 158 (15% of calories from fat), Saturated Fat: <1 g, Sodium: 304 mg

Main Dish Chicken Soup

Hearty Chili

Prep Time: 10 minutes   *Cook Time:* 20 minutes

1 tablespoon BERTOLLI® Classico Olive Oil
1 medium onion, chopped
1 medium green bell pepper, chopped
2 pounds lean ground beef
1 jar (1 pound 10 ounces) CARB OPTIONS™ Garden Style Sauce
2 tablespoons chili powder
½ teaspoon ground cumin
½ teaspoon salt
1 cup shredded cheddar cheese (about 4 ounces), optional

1. In 12-inch nonstick skillet, heat olive oil over medium-high heat and cook onion and green pepper, stirring occasionally, 3 minutes. Add ground beef and cook until brown, stirring occasionally; drain.

2. Stir in Carb Options Garden Style Sauce, chili powder, cumin and salt. Simmer uncovered, stirring occasionally, 10 minutes. Garnish with cheese.   *Makes 6 servings*

NUTRIENTS PER SERVING (⅙ of total recipe): Carbohydrate: 12 g, Fat: 28 g, Protein: 30 g, Calories: 420 (60% of calories from fat), Saturated Fat: 9 g, Sodium: 840 mg

Broccoli 'n Cheddar Soup

Prep Time: 10 minutes   *Cook Time:* 25 minutes

1 tablespoon BERTOLLI® Classico Olive Oil
1 rib celery, chopped (about ½ cup)
1 carrot, chopped (about ½ cup)
1 small onion, chopped (about ½ cup)
½ teaspoon dried thyme leaves, crushed (optional)
2 cans (14½ ounces each) chicken broth
1 jar (1 pound) CARB OPTIONS™ Double Cheddar Sauce
1 package (10 ounces) frozen chopped broccoli, thawed and drained

1. In 3-quart saucepan, heat olive oil over medium heat and cook celery, carrot, onion and thyme 3 minutes or until vegetables are almost tender. Add chicken broth and bring to a boil over high heat. Reduce heat to medium and simmer uncovered 10 minutes.

2. In food processor or blender, puree vegetable mixture until smooth; return to saucepan. Stir in Carb Options Double Cheddar Sauce and broccoli. Cook 10 minutes or until heated through.   *Makes 6 servings*

NUTRIENTS PER SERVING (1 cup): Carbohydrate: 9 g, Fat: 14 g, Protein: 7 g, Calories: 180 (70% of calories from fat), Saturated Fat: 4 g, Sodium: 1030 mg

Cioppino

Prep and Cook Time: 30 minutes

- **1 teaspoon olive oil**
- **1 large onion, chopped**
- **1 cup sliced celery, with celery tops**
- **1 clove garlic, minced**
- **4 cups water**
- **1 tablespoon salt-free Italian herb seasoning**
- **1 fish-flavored bouillon cube**
- **¼ pound cod or other boneless mild-flavored fish fillets**
- **1 large tomato, chopped**
- **1 can (10 ounces) baby clams, rinsed and drained (optional)**
- **¼ pound uncooked small shrimp, peeled and deveined**
- **¼ pound uncooked bay scallops**
- **¼ cup flaked crabmeat or crabmeat blend**
- **2 tablespoons fresh lemon juice**

1. Heat olive oil in large saucepan over medium heat until hot. Add onion, celery and garlic. Cook and stir 5 minutes or until onion is soft. Add water, Italian seasoning and bouillon cube. Cover and bring to a boil over high heat.

2. Cut fish into ½-inch pieces. Add fish and tomato to saucepan. Reduce heat to medium-low; simmer about 5 minutes or until fish is opaque. Add clams, if desired, shrimp, scallops, crabmeat and lemon juice; simmer about 5 minutes or until shrimp and scallops are opaque.   *Makes 4 servings*

NUTRIENTS PER SERVING (1¾ cups): Carbohydrate: 8 g, Fat: 2 g, Protein: 18 g, Calories: 122 (18% of calories from fat), Saturated Fat: <1 g, Sodium: 412 mg

Hot and Sour Soup

3 cans (14½ ounces each) chicken broth
8 ounces boneless skinless chicken breasts, cut into ¼-inch-thick strips
1 cup shredded carrots
1 cup thinly sliced mushrooms
½ cup bamboo shoots, cut into matchstick-size strips
2 tablespoons rice vinegar or white wine vinegar
½ to ¾ teaspoon white pepper
¼ to ½ teaspoon hot pepper sauce
2 tablespoons cornstarch
2 tablespoons soy sauce
1 tablespoon dry sherry
2 medium green onions, sliced
1 egg, lightly beaten

1. Combine chicken broth, chicken, carrots, mushrooms, bamboo shoots, vinegar, pepper and hot pepper sauce in large saucepan. Bring to a boil over medium-high heat; reduce heat to low. Cover and simmer about 5 minutes or until chicken is no longer pink.

2. Stir together cornstarch, soy sauce and sherry in small bowl until smooth. Add to chicken broth mixture. Cook and stir until mixture comes to a boil. Stir in green onions and egg. Cook about 1 minute, stirring in one direction, until egg is cooked.

Makes 7 servings

NUTRIENTS PER SERVING (1 cup): Carbohydrate: 7 g, Fat: 2 g, Protein: 8 g, Calories: 85 (21% of calories from fat), Saturated Fat: 1 g, Sodium: 1031 mg

Spicy Pumpkin Soup with Green Chili Swirl

1 can (4 ounces) diced green chilies
¼ cup reduced-fat sour cream
¼ cup fresh cilantro leaves
1 can (15 ounces) solid-pack pumpkin
1 can (14½ ounces) fat-free reduced-sodium chicken broth
½ cup water
1 teaspoon ground cumin
½ teaspoon chili powder
¼ teaspoon garlic powder
⅛ teaspoon ground red pepper (optional)
    Additional sour cream (optional)

1. Combine chilies, ¼ cup sour cream and cilantro in food processor or blender; process until smooth.

2. Combine pumpkin, broth, water, cumin, chili powder, garlic powder and red pepper, if desired, in medium saucepan; stir in ¼ cup green chili mixture. Bring to a boil; reduce heat to medium. Simmer, uncovered 5 minutes, stirring occasionally.

3. Pour into serving bowls. Top each serving with small dollops of remaining green chili mixture and additional sour cream, if desired. Run tip of spoon through dollops to swirl.

Makes 4 servings

NUTRIENTS PER SERVING (¼ of total recipe without additional sour cream):
Carbohydrate: 12 g, Fat: 1 g, Protein: 4 g, Calories: 72 (17% of calories from fat), Saturated Fat: <1 g, Sodium: 276 mg

Spicy Pumpkin Soup with Green Chili Swirl

Chicken and Vegetable Chowder

1 pound boneless skinless chicken breasts, cut into 1-inch pieces
1 bag (10 ounces) frozen cut-up broccoli
1 cup sliced carrots
1 jar (4½ ounces) sliced mushrooms, drained
½ cup chopped onion
½ cup whole kernel corn
2 cloves garlic, minced
½ teaspoon dried thyme leaves
1 can (14½ ounces) reduced-sodium chicken broth
1 can (10¾ ounces) condensed cream of potato soup
⅓ cup half-and-half

Slow Cooker Directions

1. Combine all ingredients except half-and-half in slow cooker. Cover and cook on LOW 5 hours or until vegetables are tender and chicken is no longer pink in center.

2. Stir in half-and-half. Turn to HIGH. Cover and cook 15 minutes or until heated through.

Makes 6 servings

Variation: If desired, add ½ cup (2 ounces) shredded Swiss or Cheddar cheese just before serving, stirring over LOW heat until melted.

NUTRIENTS PER SERVING (⅙ of total recipe): Carbohydrate: 15 g, Fat: 5 g, Protein: 22 g, Calories: 188 (24% of calories from fat), Saturated Fat: 1 g, Sodium: 704 mg

Chicken and Vegetable Chowder

Thai Noodle Soup

Prep and Cook Time: 15 minutes

    1 package (3 ounces) ramen noodles
    ¾ pound chicken tenders
    2 cans (14½ ounces each) chicken broth
    ¼ cup shredded carrot
    ¼ cup frozen snow peas
    2 tablespoons thinly sliced green onion tops
    ½ teaspoon minced garlic
    ¼ teaspoon ground ginger
    3 tablespoons chopped fresh cilantro
    ½ lime, cut into 4 wedges

1. Break noodles into pieces. Cook noodles according to package directions (discard flavor packet). Drain and set aside.

2. Cut chicken tenders into ½-inch pieces. Combine chicken broth and chicken tenders in large saucepan or Dutch oven; bring to a boil over medium heat. Cook 2 minutes.

3. Add carrot, snow peas, green onions, garlic and ginger. Reduce heat to low; simmer 3 minutes. Add cooked noodles and cilantro; heat through. Serve soup with lime wedges. *Makes 4 servings*

NUTRIENTS PER SERVING (¼ of total recipe): Carbohydrate: 13 g, Fat: 7 g, Protein: 23 g, Calories: 200 (32% of calories from fat), Saturated Fat: 1 g, Sodium: 900 mg

Main Events

Sirloin with Sweet Caramelized Onions

    Nonstick cooking spray
  1 medium onion, very thinly sliced
  1 boneless beef top sirloin steak (about 1 pound)
  ¼ cup water
  2 tablespoons Worcestershire sauce
  1 tablespoon sugar

1. Lightly coat 12-inch skillet with cooking spray; heat over high heat until hot. Add onion; cook and stir 4 minutes or until browned. Remove from skillet and set aside. Wipe out skillet with paper towel.

2. Coat same skillet with cooking spray; heat until hot. Add beef; cook 10 to 13 minutes for medium-rare to medium, turning once. Remove from heat and transfer to cutting board; let stand 3 minutes before slicing.

3. Meanwhile, return skillet to high heat until hot; add onion, water, Worcestershire sauce and sugar. Cook 30 to 45 seconds or until most liquid has evaporated.

4. Thinly slice beef on the diagonal and serve with onions. *Makes 4 servings*

NUTRIENTS PER SERVING (¼ of total recipe): Carbohydrate: 7 g, Fat: 5 g, Protein: 21 g, Calories: 159 (28% of calories from fat), Saturated Fat: 2 g, Sodium: 118 mg

Oven-Fried Chicken

2 boneless skinless chicken breasts (about 4 ounces each), cut into halves
4 small skinless chicken drumsticks (about 2½ ounces each)
3 tablespoons all-purpose flour
½ teaspoon poultry seasoning
¼ teaspoon garlic salt
¼ teaspoon black pepper
1½ cups cornflakes, crushed
1 tablespoon dried parsley flakes
1 egg white
1 tablespoon water
  Nonstick cooking spray

1. Preheat oven to 375°F. Rinse chicken. Trim off any fat. Pat dry with paper towels.

2. Combine flour, poultry seasoning, garlic salt and pepper in resealable plastic food storage bag. Combine cornflake crumbs and parsley in shallow bowl. Whisk together egg white and water in small bowl.

3. Add chicken to flour mixture, one or two pieces at a time. Seal bag; shake until chicken is well coated. Remove chicken from bag, shaking off excess flour. Dip into egg white mixture, coating all sides. Roll in crumb mixture. Place in shallow baking pan. Repeat with remaining chicken, flour mixture, egg white and crumb mixture.

4. Lightly spray chicken pieces with cooking spray. Bake breast pieces 18 to 20 minutes or until no longer pink in center. Bake drumsticks about 25 minutes or until juices run clear.

Makes 4 servings

NUTRIENTS PER SERVING (1 chicken breast half plus 1 drumstick):
Carbohydrate: 14 g, Fat: 4 g, Protein: 27 g, Calories: 208 (18% of calories from fat), Saturated Fat: 1 g, Sodium: 348 mg

Oven-Fried Chicken

Hot and Sour Shrimp

½ **package (½ ounce) dried black Chinese mushrooms***
½ **small unpeeled cucumber**
1 **tablespoon brown sugar**
2 **teaspoons cornstarch**
3 **tablespoons rice vinegar**
2 **tablespoons reduced-sodium soy sauce**
1 **tablespoon vegetable oil**
1 **pound medium raw shrimp, peeled and deveined**
2 **cloves garlic, minced**
¼ **teaspoon red pepper flakes**
1 **large red bell pepper, cut into short, thin strips**
   Hot cooked Chinese egg noodles (optional)

*Or substitute ¾ cup sliced fresh mushrooms. Omit step 1.

1. Place mushrooms in small bowl; cover with warm water. Soak 20 minutes to soften. Drain; squeeze out excess water. Discard stems; slice caps.

2. Cut cucumber in half lengthwise; scrape out seeds. Slice crosswise.

3. Combine brown sugar and cornstarch in small bowl. Blend in vinegar and soy sauce until smooth.

4. Heat oil in wok or large nonstick skillet over medium heat. Add shrimp, garlic and red pepper flakes; cook and stir 1 minute. Add mushrooms and bell pepper strips; cook and stir 2 minutes or until shrimp are opaque.

5. Stir vinegar mixture; add to wok. Cook and stir 30 seconds or until sauce boils and thickens. Add cucumber; stir-fry until heated through. Serve over noodles, if desired.

Makes 4 servings

NUTRIENTS PER SERVING (¼ of total recipe without noodles): Carbohydrate: 11 g, Fat: 5 g, Protein: 20 g, Calories: 165 (24% of calories from fat), Saturated Fat: <1 g, Sodium: 466 mg

Hot and Sour Shrimp

Mesquite-Grilled Salmon Fillets

2 tablespoons olive oil
1 clove garlic, minced
2 tablespoons lemon juice
1 teaspoon grated lemon peel
½ teaspoon dried dill weed
½ teaspoon dried thyme leaves
¼ teaspoon salt
¼ teaspoon black pepper
4 salmon fillets, ¾ to 1 inch thick (about 5 ounces each)

1. Cover 1 cup mesquite chips with cold water; soak 20 to 30 minutes. Prepare grill for direct cooking.

2. Combine oil and garlic in small microwavable bowl. Microwave at HIGH 1 minute or until garlic is tender. Add lemon juice, lemon peel, dill, thyme, salt and pepper; whisk until blended. Brush skinless sides of salmon with half of lemon mixture.

3. Drain mesquite chips; sprinkle chips over coals. Place salmon, skin side up, on grid. Grill, covered, over medium-high heat 4 to 5 minutes; turn and brush with remaining lemon mixture. Grill 4 to 5 minutes or until salmon flakes easily when tested with fork.

Makes 4 servings

NUTRIENTS PER SERVING (¼ of total recipe): Carbohydrate: 1 g, Fat: 22 g, Protein: 28 g, Calories: 322 (65% of calories from fat), Saturated Fat: 4 g, Sodium: 230 mg

Mesquite-Grilled Salmon Fillet

Crispy Oven Fried Fish Fingers

½ cup seasoned dry bread crumbs
1 tablespoon grated Parmesan cheese
2 teaspoons grated lemon peel
¾ teaspoon dried marjoram leaves
½ teaspoon paprika
¼ teaspoon dried thyme leaves
⅛ teaspoon garlic powder
4 cod fillets (about 1 pound)
3 tablespoons lemon juice
2 tablespoons water
1 tablespoon CRISCO® Oil*

Use your favorite Crisco Oil product.

1. Heat oven to 425°F. Oil 13×9×2-inch pan lightly. Place cooling rack on countertop.

2. Combine bread crumbs, Parmesan cheese, lemon peel, marjoram, paprika, thyme and garlic powder in shallow dish.

3. Rinse fish fillets and pat dry.

4. Combine lemon juice and water in separate shallow dish. Cut fish into desired size "fingers" or "sticks." Dip each fish finger into lemon mixture, then into crumb mixture, coating well. Place in pan. Drizzle with oil.

5. Bake at 425°F for 10 to 12 minutes or until fish flakes easily with fork. *Do not overbake.* Remove to cooling rack. Let stand 2 to 3 minutes in pan. Remove to serving plate. Garnish, if desired.   *Makes 4 servings*

NUTRIENTS PER SERVING (¼ of total recipe): Carbohydrate: 7 g, Fat: 6 g, Protein: 24 g, Calories: 175 (28% of calories from fat), Saturated Fat: 1 g, Sodium: 180 mg

Chicken Carbonara

Prep Time: 5 minutes   *Cook Time:* 20 minutes

   1 tablespoon BERTOLLI® Classico Olive Oil
   4 boneless, skinless chicken breast halves (about 1 pound)
   1 small onion, chopped
   1 slice bacon, chopped
   ⅓ cup chicken broth
   1 jar (1 pound) CARB OPTIONS™ Alfredo Sauce

1. In 12-inch nonstick skillet, heat olive oil over medium-high heat and brown chicken. Remove chicken and set aside.

2. In same skillet, cook onion and bacon over medium heat, stirring occasionally, 6 minutes or until bacon is cooked. Add broth and cook 1 minute. Stir in Carb Options Alfredo Sauce. Bring to a boil over high heat. Reduce heat to low, then return chicken to skillet. Simmer covered 5 minutes or until chicken is thoroughly cooked.

Makes 4 servings

NUTRIENTS PER SERVING (¼ of total recipe): Carbohydrate: 6 g, Fat: 28 g, Protein: 34 g, Calories: 410 (61% of calories from fat), Saturated Fat: 9 g, Sodium: 970 mg

Turkey Cutlets with Victory Garden Gravy

Prep Time: 15 minutes

1 package BUTTERBALL® Fresh Boneless Turkey Breast Cutlets
½ cup milk
3 tablespoons flour
1 can (14½ ounces) chicken broth
2 cups broccoli florets
½ cup chopped plum tomatoes
1 tablespoon chopped fresh parsley
¼ teaspoon salt
¼ teaspoon black pepper
1 tablespoon vegetable oil
2 tablespoons grated Parmesan cheese

Whisk together milk and flour in small bowl. Combine milk mixture and chicken broth in large saucepan. Bring to a boil over medium-high heat, stirring constantly. Reduce heat to low; add broccoli. Simmer 5 minutes. Stir in tomatoes, parsley, salt and pepper. Heat oil in separate large skillet over medium heat until hot. Cook cutlets 2 to 2½ minutes on each side or until no longer pink in center. Serve with gravy. Sprinkle with Parmesan cheese.

Makes 4 servings

NUTRIENTS PER SERVING (¼ of total recipe): Carbohydrate: 10 g, Fat: 3.5 g, Protein: 25 g, Calories: 197 (14% of calories from fat), Saturated Fat: 2 g, Sodium: 730 mg

Turkey Cutlets with Victory Garden Gravy

Oriental Flank Steak

Prep Time: 5 minutes   *Cook Time:* 15 minutes   *Marinate Time:* 3 hours

- ¾ **cup WISH-BONE® Italian Dressing***
- **3 tablespoons soy sauce**
- **3 tablespoons firmly packed brown sugar**
- ½ **teaspoon ground ginger (optional)**
- **1 to 1½ pounds flank, top round or sirloin steak**

*Also terrific with Wish-Bone® Robusto Italian, Lite Italian or Red Wine Vinaigrette Dressing.

In small bowl, combine all ingredients except steak.

In large, shallow nonaluminum baking dish or plastic bag, pour ½ cup marinade over steak. Cover, or close bag, and marinate in refrigerator, turning occasionally, 3 to 24 hours. Refrigerate remaining marinade.

Remove steak from marinade, discarding marinade. Grill or broil steak, turning once and brushing frequently with reserved marinade, until steak is desired doneness.

Makes about 4 servings

NUTRIENTS PER SERVING (¼ of total recipe): Carbohydrate: 4 g, Fat: 10 g, Protein: 20 g, Calories: 190 (47% of calories from fat), Saturated Fat: 4 g, Sodium: 430 mg

Oriental Flank Steak

Spinach, Cheese and Prosciutto-Stuffed Chicken Breasts

4 boneless skinless chicken breasts (about 4 ounces each)
   Salt and black pepper
4 slices (½ ounce each) prosciutto*
4 slices (½ ounce each) smoked provolone**
1 cup spinach leaves, chopped
4 tablespoons all-purpose flour, divided
1 tablespoon olive oil
1 tablespoon butter
1 cup chicken broth
1 tablespoon heavy cream

Thinly sliced deli ham can be substituted for the prosciutto.

Swiss, Gruyére or mozzarella cheese may be substituted for the smoked provolone.

1. Preheat oven to 350°F.

2. To form pocket, cut each chicken breast horizontally almost to opposite edge. Fold back top half of chicken breast; sprinkle chicken lightly with salt and pepper. Place 1 slice prosciutto, 1 slice provolone and ¼ cup spinach on each chicken breast. Fold top half of breasts over filling.

3. Spread 3 tablespoons flour on plate. Holding chicken breast closed, coat with flour; shake off excess. Lightly sprinkle chicken with salt and pepper.

4. Heat oil and butter in large skillet over medium heat. Place chicken in skillet; cook about 4 minutes on each side or until browned.

5. Transfer chicken to shallow baking dish. Bake in oven 10 minutes or until chicken is no longer pink in center and juices run clear.

6. Whisk chicken broth and cream into remaining 1 tablespoon flour in small bowl. Pour chicken broth mixture into same skillet; heat over medium heat, stirring constantly, until

continued on page 110

Spinach, Cheese and Prosciutto-Stuffed Chicken Breast

Spinach, Cheese and Prosciutto-Stuffed Chicken Breast, continued

sauce thickens, about 3 minutes. Spoon sauce onto serving plates; top with chicken breasts. *Makes 4 servings*

Tip: Prosciutto, an Italian ham, is seasoned, cured and air-dried, not smoked. Look for imported or less expensive domestic prosciutto in delis and Italian food markets.

NUTRIENTS PER SERVING (¼ of total recipe): Carbohydrate: 7 g, Fat: 23 g, Protein: 33 g, Calories: 371 (57% of calories from fat), Saturated Fat: 9 g, Sodium: 854 mg

Almond Parmesan Chicken

Prep Time: 15 minutes   *Marinate Time:* 30 minutes   *Cook Time:* 16 minutes

- **4 boneless, skinless chicken breast halves (about 1 pound)**
- **½ cup CARB OPTIONS™ Italian Garlic Marinade**
- **2 tablespoons sliced or slivered almonds**
- **3 tablespoons freshly grated Parmesan cheese**
- **1 tablespoon BERTOLLI® Extra Virgin Olive Oil**
- **1 tablespoon finely chopped basil**

1. In large self-closing plastic bag, combine chicken and Carb Options Italian Garlic Marinade. Marinate chicken in refrigerator for 30 minutes. Remove chicken from bag, discarding used Marinade.

2. Broil chicken until thoroughly cooked, about 8 minutes per side. Top chicken with almonds and Parmesan. Broil just until cheese is melted, watching carefully. Drizzle with olive oil and sprinkle basil over the chicken. *Makes 4 servings*

NUTRIENTS PER SERVING (¼ of total recipe): Carbohydrate: 2 g, Fat: 10 g, Protein: 26 g, Calories: 210 (43% of calories from fat), Saturated Fat: 2 g, Sodium: 730 mg

Pulled BBQ Pork

Prep Time: 10 minutes   *Cook Time:* 6 hours

6- to 7-pound pork butt
3 tablespoons LAWRY'S® Seasoned Salt
2 bottles (13.1 ounces each) CARB OPTIONS™ Hickory Barbecue Sauce
Romaine hearts
Latino Slaw (page 164)

1. Preheat oven to 275°F. Place pork butt on 13×9-inch baking dish. Rub with Seasoned Salt, then cover tightly with aluminum foil. Cook 6 hours or until meat is very tender and almost falls off the bone (about 1 hour per pound). Remove from oven and let stand covered 15 minutes.

2. With a fork in each hand, shred the pork in the baking dish (reserve 1 cup juices in the dish, draining off fat and removing any large pieces of fat or gristle). In a 4-quart saucepot, combine shredded pork, Carb Options Hickory Barbecue Sauce and reserved 1 cup juice. Cook over medium-low heat, stirring occasionally, 15 minutes.

3. Trim and discard outer leaves of romaine and cut the bottoms. Wash hearts in cold water and dry with paper towel. To serve, top each romaine leaf with about 2 tablespoons pulled pork. Serve with Latino Slaw.   *Makes 16 servings*

NUTRIENTS PER SERVING (¹⁄₁₆ of total recipe without slaw): Carbohydrate: 3 g, Fat: 16 g, Protein: 17 g, Calories: 220 (65% of calories from fat), Saturated Fat: 6 g, Sodium: 1360 mg

Crustless Southwestern Quiche

8 ounces chorizo sausage*

8 eggs

1 package (10 ounces) frozen chopped spinach, thawed and squeezed dry

1 cup crumbled queso fresco or 1 cup (4 ounces) shredded Cheddar or pepper Jack cheese

½ cup whipping cream or half-and-half

¼ cup salsa

*Substitute 8 ounces bulk pork sausage plus ¼ teaspoon ground red pepper if chorizo is not available.

1. Preheat oven to 400°F. Grease 10-inch quiche dish or deep-dish pie plate.

2. Remove sausage from casings. Crumble sausage into medium skillet. Cook over medium heat until sausage is browned, stirring to break up meat. Remove from heat; pour off drippings. Cool 5 minutes.

3. Beat eggs in medium bowl. Add spinach, cheese, cream and sausage; mix well. Pour into prepared quiche dish. Bake 20 minutes or until center is set. Let stand 5 minutes before cutting into wedges. Serve with salsa.   *Makes 4 servings*

NUTRIENTS PER SERVING (¼ of total recipe): Carbohydrate: 9 g, Fat: 45 g, Protein: 36 g, Calories: 583 (69% of calories from fat), Saturated Fat: 18 g, Sodium: 922 mg

Crustless Southwestern Quiche

Flounder Fillets with Carrots

1 pound carrots, julienned (about 4 large)
2 tablespoons minced parsley
1 teaspoon olive oil
⅛ teaspoon salt
⅛ teaspoon pepper
4 (4- to 5-ounce) flounder fillets*
2 teaspoons coarse-grain Dijon mustard
1 teaspoon honey

Or, substitute other fish fillets, such as tilapia, sole, cod, catfish, halibut, ocean perch, trout, orange roughy or pollock.

Combine carrots, parsley, oil, salt and pepper in 11×7-inch microwavable baking dish. Cover with waxed paper. Microwave at HIGH 5 minutes, stirring once.

Fold thin fillets in half to give all fillets even thickness. Place fillets over carrots with thick parts toward corners of dish. Combine mustard and honey; spread over fillets.

Cover with waxed paper. Microwave at HIGH 2 minutes. Rotate fillets, placing cooked parts toward center; continue to cook 1 to 3 minutes longer or just until fish flakes easily when tested with a fork. Let stand, covered, 2 minutes. Arrange fish and carrots on warm plates.
Makes 4 servings

Favorite recipe from **National Fisheries Institute**

NUTRIENTS PER SERVING (¼ of total recipe): Carbohydrate: 14 g, Fat: 3 g, Protein: 23 g, Calories: 173 (15% of calories from fat), Saturated Fat: 1 g, Sodium: 254 mg

Flounder Fillet with Carrots

Classic Grilled Chicken

1 whole frying chicken* (3½ pounds), quartered
¼ cup lemon juice
¼ cup olive oil
2 tablespoons soy sauce
2 large cloves garlic, minced
½ teaspoon sugar
½ teaspoon ground cumin
¼ teaspoon black pepper

Substitute 3½ pounds chicken parts for whole chicken, if desired. Grill legs and thighs about 35 minutes and breast halves about 25 minutes or until chicken is no longer pink in center, turning once.

Rinse chicken under cold running water; pat dry with paper towels. Arrange chicken in 13×9×2-inch glass baking dish. Combine remaining ingredients in small bowl; pour half of mixture over chicken. Cover and refrigerate chicken at least 1 hour or overnight. Cover and reserve remaining mixture in refrigerator to use for basting. Remove chicken from marinade; discard marinade. Arrange medium KINGSFORD® Briquets on each side of large rectangular metal or foil drip pan. Pour hot tap water into drip pan until half full. Place chicken on grid directly above drip pan. Grill chicken, skin side down, on covered grill 25 minutes. Baste with reserved mixture. Turn chicken; cook 20 to 25 minutes or until juices run clear and chicken is no longer pink in center. *Makes 6 servings*

NUTRIENTS PER SERVING (⅙ of total recipe without skin): Carbohydrate: 1 g, Fat: 30 g, Protein: 29 g, Calories: 299 (69% of calories from fat), Saturated Fat: 8 g, Sodium: 298 mg

Classic Grilled Chicken

Pork Schnitzel

Prep and Cook Time: 20 minutes

4 boneless pork chops, ¼ inch thick (3 ounces each)
½ cup corn flake crumbs or cracker crumbs
1 egg, lightly beaten
   Black pepper
2 to 4 teaspoons olive oil, divided
⅓ cup lemon juice
¼ cup chicken broth

1. Preheat oven to 200°F. Place ovenproof platter or baking sheet in oven. Trim fat from pork chops; discard fat. Place pork chops between layers of waxed paper; pound with smooth side of mallet to ⅛-inch thickness. Place crumbs in medium bowl. Dip 1 pork chop at a time in egg; gently shake off excess. Dip in crumbs to coat both sides. Place breaded pork chops in single layer on plate. Sprinkle with pepper.

2. Heat 2 teaspoons oil in large skillet over medium-high heat until hot. Add pork chops in single layer. Cook 1 minute or until golden brown on bottom. Turn and cook ½ to 1 minute or until golden brown and pork is no longer pink in center. Transfer to platter in oven. Repeat with remaining pork chops, adding oil as needed to prevent meat from sticking to skillet.

3. Remove skillet from heat. Add lemon juice and broth. Stir to scrape cooked bits from pan bottom. Return to heat; bring to a boil, stirring constantly, until liquid is reduced to 3 to 4 tablespoons. Remove platter from oven. Pour lemon juice mixture over meat. Garnish as desired.   *Makes 4 servings*

NUTRIENTS PER SERVING (¼ of total recipe): Carbohydrate: 5 g, Fat: 10 g, Protein: 18 g, Calories: 188 (49% of calories from fat), Saturated Fat: 3 g, Sodium: 161 mg

Pork Schnitzel

Italian Herb Chicken

Prep Time: 10 minutes   *Marinate Time:* 30 minutes   *Cook Time:* 50 minutes

3 pounds chicken parts
¾ cup CARB OPTIONS™ Italian Garlic Marinade
1½ teaspoons LAWRY'S® Lemon Pepper
2 tablespoons chopped fresh flat-leaf parsley
¼ teaspoon crushed red pepper flakes (optional)

1. In large self-closing plastic bag, combine chicken and Carb Options Italian Garlic Marinade. Marinate chicken in refrigerator for 30 minutes. Remove chicken from bag, discarding used Marinade.

2. On foil-lined jelly-roll pan or baking dish, place chicken skin-side up. Bake in 350°F oven for 45 to 50 minutes, or until chicken is thoroughly cooked. Place cooked chicken on serving platter and drizzle with pan juices. Sprinkle with Lemon Pepper, parsley and red pepper flakes.

Makes 6 servings

NUTRIENTS PER SERVING (⅙ of total recipe): Carbohydrate: 1 g, Fat: 12 g, Protein: 25 g, Calories: 220 (49% of calories from fat), Saturated Fat: 4 g, Sodium: 470 mg

Beef Bourguignon

1 to 2 boneless beef top sirloin steaks (about 3 pounds)
½ cup all-purpose flour
4 slices bacon, diced
2 medium carrots, diced
8 small new red potatoes, unpeeled, cut into quarters
8 to 10 mushrooms, sliced
20 to 24 pearl onions
3 cloves garlic, minced
1 bay leaf
1 teaspoon dried marjoram leaves
½ teaspoon dried thyme leaves
½ teaspoon salt
   Black pepper
2½ cups Burgundy wine or beef broth

Slow Cooker Directions

1. Cut beef into ½-inch pieces. Coat with flour, shaking off excess; set aside.

2. Cook bacon in large skillet over medium heat until partially cooked. Add beef; cook until browned. Remove beef and bacon with slotted spoon.

3. Layer carrots, potatoes, mushrooms, onions, garlic, bay leaf, marjoram, thyme, salt, pepper to taste and beef and bacon mixture in slow cooker. Pour wine over all. Cover; cook on LOW 8 to 9 hours or until beef is tender. Remove bay leaf and discard before serving. *Makes 10 servings*

NUTRIENTS PER SERVING (¹⁄₁₀ of total recipe, about 1 bowl): Carbohydrate: 14 g, Fat: 7 g, Protein: 26 g, Calories: 268 (23% of calories from fat), Saturated Fat: 3 g, Sodium: 287 mg

Cajun Grilled Shrimp

3 green onions, minced
2 tablespoons lemon juice
3 cloves garlic, minced
2 teaspoons paprika
1 teaspoon salt
$\frac{1}{4}$ to $\frac{1}{2}$ teaspoon black pepper
$\frac{1}{4}$ to $\frac{1}{2}$ teaspoon cayenne pepper
1 tablespoon olive oil
1$\frac{1}{2}$ pounds shrimp, shelled with tails intact, deveined
Lemon wedges

Combine onions, lemon juice, garlic, paprika, salt and peppers in 2-quart glass dish; stir in oil. Add shrimp; turn to coat. Cover and refrigerate at least 15 minutes. Thread shrimp onto metal or wooden skewers. (Soak wooden skewers in hot water 30 minutes to prevent burning.) Grill shrimp over medium-hot KINGSFORD® Briquets about 2 minutes per side until opaque. Serve immediately with lemon wedges. *Makes 4 servings*

NUTRIENTS PER SERVING ($\frac{1}{4}$ of total recipe): Carbohydrate: 3 g, Fat: 5 g, Protein: 28 g, Calories: 173 (27% of calories from fat), Saturated Fat: 1 g, Sodium: 882 mg

Cajun Grilled Shrimp

Grilled Fish with Orange-Chile Salsa

3 medium oranges, peeled and sectioned* (about 1¼ cups segments)
¼ cup finely diced green, red or yellow bell pepper
3 tablespoons chopped cilantro, divided
3 tablespoons lime juice, divided
1 tablespoon honey
1 teaspoon minced, seeded serrano pepper** *or* 1 tablespoon minced jalapeño pepper
1¼ pounds firm white fish fillets, such as orange roughy, lingcod, halibut or red snapper
Lime slices
Zucchini ribbons, cooked

Canned mandarin orange segments can be substituted for fresh orange segments, if desired.

**Chile peppers can sting and irritate the skin; wear rubber gloves when handling peppers and do not touch eyes. Wash hands after handling peppers.*

To prepare Orange-Chile Salsa, combine orange segments, bell pepper, 2 tablespoons cilantro, 2 tablespoons lime juice, honey and serrano pepper. Set aside.

Season fish fillets with remaining 1 tablespoon cilantro and 1 tablespoon lime juice. Lightly oil grid to prevent sticking. Grill fish on covered grill over medium KINGSFORD® Briquets 5 minutes. Turn and top with lime slices, if desired. Grill about 5 minutes until fish flakes easily when tested with fork. Serve with Orange-Chile Salsa. Garnish with zucchini ribbons.   *Makes 4 servings*

Note: Allow about 10 minutes grilling time per inch thickness of fish fillets.

NUTRIENTS PER SERVING (¼ of total recipe): Carbohydrate: 14 g, Fat: 1 g, Protein: 21 g, Calories: 154 (7% of calories from fat), Saturated Fat: <1 g, Sodium: 88 mg

Grilled Fish with Orange-Chile Salsa

Chicken Rollatini Alfredo

Prep Time: 10 minutes   *Cook Time:* 25 minutes

6 boneless, skinless chicken breast halves (about 1½ pounds), pounded ¼ inch thick
6 thin slices prosciutto or boiled ham
6 thin slices provolone cheese
1 tablespoon BERTOLLI® Classico Olive Oil
2 tablespoons Italian seasoned dry bread crumbs
2 tablespoons grated Parmesan cheese
1 jar (1 pound) CARB OPTIONS™ Alfredo Sauce

1. Preheat oven to 400°F.

2. Season chicken, if desired, with salt and ground black pepper. Evenly top each chicken breast with slice of prosciutto, then provolone cheese; roll up and secure with wooden toothpicks. Brush chicken with olive oil, then coat with bread crumbs mixed with Parmesan cheese. On baking sheet, arrange chicken and bake 25 minutes or until chicken is thoroughly cooked.

3. Meanwhile, in medium saucepan, heat Carb Options Alfredo Sauce. To serve, remove toothpicks and spoon heated Sauce onto serving platter. Slice chicken rollatini and arrange over Sauce.

Makes 6 servings

NUTRIENTS PER SERVING (⅙ of total recipe): Carbohydrate: 6 g, Fat: 27 g, Protein: 39 g, Calories: 430 (57% of calories from fat), Saturated Fat: 11 g, Sodium: 1310 mg

Grilled Chicken

Prep Time: 5 minutes   *Cook Time:* 25 minutes

2½- to 3-pound chicken, cut into serving pieces
1 cup CARB OPTIONS™ Original Barbecue Sauce

Grill or broil chicken, brushing frequently with Carb Options Original Barbecue Sauce, until chicken is thoroughly cooked.   *Makes 4 servings*

NUTRIENTS PER SERVING (¼ of total recipe): Carbohydrate: 3 g, Fat: 15 g, Protein: 30 g, Calories: 280 (48% of calories from fat), Saturated Fat: 4 g, Sodium: 770 mg

Slow Cooked Barbecued Beef Brisket

Prep Time: 5 minutes   *Cook Time:* 8 hours

2½- to 3-pound beef brisket
1 bottle (12.9 ounces) CARB OPTIONS™ Original Barbecue Sauce

Place brisket in slow cooker fat side up. Pour Carb Options Original Barbecue Sauce over beef. Cook on low until beef is tender, 8 to 10 hours (5 to 6 hours on high). Remove beef to platter and remove fat if necessary. To serve, top sliced or shredded beef with sauce.
                                      Makes 6 servings

NUTRIENTS PER SERVING (⅙ of total recipe): Carbohydrate: 3 g, Fat: 34 g, Protein: 35 g, Calories: 470 (65% of calories from fat), Saturated Fat: 13 g, Sodium: 730 mg

Tex-Mex Pork Kabobs with Chili Sour Cream Sauce

2¼ teaspoons chili powder, divided
1¾ teaspoons cumin, divided
¾ teaspoon garlic powder, divided
¾ teaspoon onion powder, divided
¾ teaspoon dried oregano leaves, divided
1 pork tenderloin (1½ pounds), trimmed and cut into 1-inch pieces
1 cup reduced-fat sour cream
¾ teaspoon salt
¼ teaspoon black pepper
1 large red bell pepper, cored, seeded and cut into small chunks
1 large green bell pepper, cored, seeded and cut into small chunks
1 large yellow bell pepper, cored, seeded and cut into small chunks

1. Combine 1½ teaspoons chili powder, 1 teaspoon cumin, ½ teaspoon garlic powder, ½ teaspoon onion powder and ½ teaspoon oregano in medium bowl. Add pork; toss until well coated. Cover tightly and refrigerate 2 to 3 hours.

2. Combine sour cream, ¼ teaspoon salt, pepper and remaining ¾ teaspoons chili powder, ¾ teaspoon cumin, ¼ teaspoon garlic powder, ¼ teaspoon onion powder and ¼ teaspoon oregano in small bowl. Mix well. Cover tightly and refrigerate 2 to 3 hours.

3. If using wooden skewers, soak in water 20 minutes before using. Preheat grill or broiler.

4. Toss pork with remaining ½ teaspoon salt. Thread meat and peppers onto skewers. Grill over medium-hot coals 10 minutes until meat is no longer pink in center, turning several times. If broiling, place skewers on foil-lined baking sheet. Broil 8 inches from heat 5 minutes per side until no longer pink in center, turning once. Serve immediately with sour cream sauce. *Makes 4 to 6 servings*

NUTRIENTS PER SERVING (¼ of total recipe): Carbohydrate: 12 g, Fat: 12 g, Protein: 40 g, Calories: 320 (33% of calories from fat), Saturated Fat: 6 g, Sodium: 564 mg

Tex-Mex Pork Kabobs with Chili Sour Cream Sauce

Chicken Stir-Fry

Prep Time: 5 minutes   *Cook Time:* 12 minutes

4 boneless skinless chicken breast halves (about 1½ pounds)
2 tablespoons vegetable oil
2 tablespoons orange juice
2 tablespoons light soy sauce
1 tablespoon cornstarch
1 bag (16 ounces) BIRDS EYE® frozen Farm Fresh Mixtures Broccoli, Carrots & Water
   Chestnuts

• Cut chicken into ½-inch-thick long strips.

• In wok or large skillet, heat oil over medium-high heat.

• Add chicken; cook 5 minutes, stirring occasionally.

• Meanwhile, in small bowl, combine orange juice, soy sauce and cornstarch; blend well and set aside.

• Add vegetables to chicken; cook 5 minutes more or until chicken is no longer pink in center, stirring occasionally.

• Stir in soy sauce mixture; cook 1 minute or until heated through.   *Makes 4 servings*

NUTRIENTS PER SERVING (¼ of total recipe): Carbohydrate: 9 g, Fat: 9 g,
Protein: 41 g, Calories: 300 (28% of calories from fat), Saturated Fat: 1 g, Sodium: 399 mg

Chicken Stir-Fry

Southwest Skillet

Prep Time: 5 minutes   *Cook Time:* 15 minutes

1 bag (16 ounces) BIRDS EYE® frozen Pasta Secrets Zesty Garlic
1 cup cubed cooked chicken breast
1 cup chunky salsa
½ teaspoon chili powder
½ cup chopped green or red bell pepper

• In large skillet, combine all ingredients.

• Cook over medium heat 10 to 15 minutes or until heated through.   *Makes 4 servings*

Cheesy Southwest Skillet: Stir in ½ cup shredded Cheddar cheese during last 5 minutes. Cook until cheese is melted.

Creamy Southwest Skillet: Remove skillet from heat. Stir in ¼ cup sour cream before serving.

NUTRIENTS PER SERVING (¼ of total recipe): Carbohydrate: 4 g, Fat: 9 g, Protein: 39 g, Calories: 276 (32% of calories from fat), Saturated Fat: 2 g, Sodium: 706 mg

Southwest Skillet

Blackened Sea Bass

Hardwood charcoal*
2 teaspoons paprika
1 teaspoon garlic salt
1 teaspoon dried thyme leaves, crushed
$\frac{1}{4}$ teaspoon white pepper
$\frac{1}{4}$ teaspoon ground red pepper
$\frac{1}{4}$ teaspoon black pepper
3 tablespoons butter or margarine
4 skinless sea bass or catfish fillets (4 to 6 ounces each)
Lemon halves
Fresh dill sprigs for garnish

Hardwood charcoal takes somewhat longer than regular charcoal to become hot, but results in a hotter fire than regular charcoal. A hot fire is necessary to seal in juices and cook fish quickly. If hardwood charcoal is not available, scatter dry hardwood, mesquite or hickory chunks over hot coals to create a hot fire.

1. Prepare grill for direct cooking using hardwood charcoal.

2. Meanwhile, combine paprika, garlic salt, thyme and white, red and black peppers in small bowl; mix well. Set aside. Melt butter in small saucepan over medium heat. Pour melted butter into pie plate or shallow bowl. Cool slightly.

3. Dip sea bass into melted butter, evenly coating both sides. Sprinkle both sides of fish evenly with paprika mixture.

4. Place fish on grid. (Fire will flare up when fish is placed on grid, but will subside when grill is covered.) Grill fish, on covered grill, over hot coals 4 to 6 minutes or until

continued on page 136

Blackened Sea Bass

Blackened Sea Bass, continued

fish is blackened and flakes easily when tested with fork, turning halfway through grilling time. Serve with lemon halves. Garnish, if desired.   *Makes 4 servings*

NUTRIENTS PER SERVING (¼ of total recipe): Carbohydrate: 1 g, Fat: 12 g, Protein: 21 g, Calories: 195 (54% of calories from fat), Saturated Fat: 6 g, Sodium: 411 mg

Chicken Alfredo with Broccoli

Prep Time: 20 minutes   *Cook Time:* 25 minutes

- **1 tablespoon I CAN'T BELIEVE IT'S NOT BUTTER!® Spread**
- **1 medium onion, chopped**
- **1 pound boneless, skinless chicken breasts, cut into 1-inch pieces**
- **2 cups fresh or frozen broccoli florets**
- **1 jar (1 pound) CARB OPTIONS™ Alfredo Sauce**
- **⅛ teaspoon ground black pepper**

1. In 12-inch skillet, heat I Can't Believe It's Not Butter! Spread over medium-high heat and cook onion, stirring occasionally, 10 minutes or until golden.

2. Stir in chicken and continue cooking, stirring occasionally, 5 minutes. Stir in broccoli, Carb Options Alfredo Sauce and ground black pepper. Reduce heat to medium and simmer uncovered, stirring occasionally, 10 minutes or until chicken is thoroughly cooked and broccoli is tender.   *Makes 4 servings*

NUTRIENTS PER SERVING (¼ of total recipe): Carbohydrate: 9 g, Fat: 25 g, Protein: 28 g, Calories: 370 (61% of calories from fat), Saturated Fat: 8 g, Sodium: 820 mg

Grilled Steak

Prep Time: 5 minutes   *Cook Time:* 12 minutes

**4 boneless sirloin or ribeye steaks (about 5 ounces each)
CARB OPTIONS™ Steak Sauce**

Season steak, if desired, with salt and ground black pepper. Grill or broil until desired doneness. Serve with Carb Options Steak Sauce.   *Makes 4 servings*

NUTRIENTS PER SERVING (¼ of total recipe): Carbohydrate: 1 g, Fat: 5 g, Protein: 23 g, Calories: 150 (30% of calories from fat), Saturated Fat: 2 g, Sodium: 250 mg

"Spaghetti" Toss Alfredo

Prep Time: 15 minutes

1 spaghetti squash (about 2¼ pounds), halved lengthwise, seeded and cooked*
1 jar (1 pound) CARB OPTIONS™ Alfredo Sauce, heated

*In microwave-safe baking dish, microwave squash, cut side down, at HIGH, turning dish occassionally, 15 minutes or until fork tender. Or bake at 350°F for about 1 hour or until fork tender.

With fork, gently remove spaghetti-like strands from squash. Top with Carb Options Alfredo Sauce.   *Makes 5 servings*

NUTRIENTS PER SERVING (⅕ of total recipe): Carbohydrate: 14 g, Fat: 16 g, Protein: 3 g, Calories: 210 (69% of calories from fat), Saturated Fat: 6 g, Sodium: 610 mg

Round Out a Plate

Light Chicken Vegetable Salad

1¼ pounds skinless chicken breasts, cooked and cut into ¾-inch pieces
⅓ cup chopped zucchini
⅓ cup chopped carrot
2 tablespoons chopped onion
2 tablespoons chopped fresh parsley
⅓ cup fat-free mayonnaise
¼ cup fat-free sour cream
¼ teaspoon salt
⅛ teaspoon pepper
  Kale or lettuce leaves (optional)
3 tomatoes, cut into wedges
¼ cup sliced almonds, toasted

1. Combine chicken, zucchini, carrot, onion and parsley in large bowl.

2. Combine mayonnaise, sour cream, salt and pepper in small bowl. Add to chicken mixture; mix well. Cover and refrigerate at least 2 hours.

3. Line plates with kale leaves, if desired. Divide salad evenly among plates. Surround with tomato wedges; sprinkle with almonds. Garnish, if desired.   *Makes 6 servings*

NUTRIENTS PER SERVING (about ¾ cup salad with ½ tomato and 2 teaspoons almonds): Carbohydrate: 9 g, Fat: 4 g, Protein: 24 g, Calories: 178 (22% of calories from fat), Saturated Fat: 1 g, Sodium: 274 mg

Broccoli with Creamy Lemon Sauce

2 tablespoons fat-free mayonnaise
4½ teaspoons reduced-fat sour cream
1 tablespoon fat-free (skim) milk
1 to 1½ teaspoons lemon juice
⅛ teaspoon ground turmeric
1¼ cups hot cooked broccoli florets

Combine all ingredients except broccoli in top of double boiler. Cook over simmering water 5 minutes or until heated through, stirring constantly. Serve over hot cooked broccoli.   *Makes 2 servings*

NUTRIENTS PER SERVING (½ of total recipe): Carbohydrate: 7 g, Fat: 1 g, Protein: 2 g, Calories: 44 (18% of calories from fat), Saturated Fat: <1 g, Sodium: 216 mg

Dilled Brussels Sprouts

1 package (10 ounces) frozen brussels sprouts *or* 1 pint fresh brussels sprouts
½ cup fat-free beef broth
1 teaspoon dill seed
1 teaspoon instant minced onion (optional)
Salt and pepper to taste (optional)

Combine all ingredients in saucepan; simmer, covered, 8 to 10 minutes, or until sprouts are nearly tender. Uncover and continue to simmer until most of the liquid has evaporated.   *Makes 3 servings*

NUTRIENTS PER SERVING (⅓ of total recipe): Carbohydrate: 8 g, Fat: 1 g, Protein: 4 g, Calories: 43 (10% of calories from fat), Saturated Fat: <1 g, Sodium: 23 mg

Broccoli with Creamy Lemon Sauce

Jalapeño Wild Rice Cakes

$^1/_3$ **cup wild rice**
$^3/_4$ **cup water**
$^1/_2$ **teaspoon salt, divided**
 1 **tablespoon all-purpose flour**
$^1/_2$ **teaspoon baking powder**
 1 **egg**
 1 **jalapeño pepper,* finely chopped**
 2 **tablespoons minced onion**
 1 **tablespoon freshly grated ginger** *or* **2 teaspoons ground ginger**
 2 **tablespoons vegetable or olive oil**

*Jalapeño peppers can sting and irritate the skin. Wear rubber gloves when handling peppers and do not touch eyes. Wash hands after handling.

1. Combine rice, water and $^1/_4$ teaspoon salt in medium saucepan. Bring to a boil. Reduce heat; cover and simmer 40 to 45 minutes or until rice is tender. Drain rice, if necessary; place in medium bowl. Add flour, baking powder and remaining $^1/_4$ teaspoon salt; mix until blended.

2. Whisk together egg, jalapeño pepper, onion and ginger in small bowl. Pour egg mixture over rice; mix until well blended.

3. Heat oil in large nonstick skillet over medium heat. Spoon 2 tablespoons rice mixture into pan and shape into 3-inch cake. Cook, 4 cakes at a time, 3 minutes on each side or until golden brown. Transfer to paper towels. Serve immediately or refrigerate up to 24 hours.   *Makes 8 rice cakes*

Tip: To reheat cold rice cakes, preheat oven to 400°F. Place rice cakes in single layer on baking sheet; heat 5 minutes.

NUTRIENTS PER SERVING (1 rice cake): Carbohydrate: 6 g, Fat: 4 g, Protein: 2 g, Calories: 63 (57% of calories from fat), Saturated Fat: <1 g, Sodium: 330 mg

Jalapeño Wild Rice Cakes

Polenta Triangles

½ **cup yellow corn grits**
1½ **cups fat-free reduced-sodium chicken broth, divided**
2 **cloves garlic, minced**
½ **cup (2 ounces) crumbled feta cheese**
1 **red bell pepper, roasted,* peeled and finely chopped**

*Place pepper on foil-lined broiler pan; broil 15 minutes or until blackened on all sides, turning every 5 minutes. Place pepper in paper bag; close bag and let stand 15 minutes before peeling.

1. Combine grits and ½ cup chicken broth in small bowl; mix well and set aside. Pour remaining 1 cup broth into large heavy saucepan; bring to a boil. Add garlic and moistened grits; mix well and return to a boil. Reduce heat to low; cover and cook 20 minutes. Remove from heat; add feta cheese. Stir until cheese is completely melted. Add roasted bell pepper; mix well.

2. Spray 8-inch square pan with nonstick cooking spray. Spoon grits mixture into prepared pan. Press grits evenly into pan with wet fingertips. Refrigerate until cold.

3. Spray grid with nonstick cooking spray. Prepare grill for direct cooking. Turn polenta out onto cutting board and cut into 2-inch squares. Cut each square diagonally into 2 triangles.

4. Place polenta triangles on grid. Grill over medium-high heat 1 minute or until bottoms are lightly browned. Turn triangles over and grill until browned and crisp. Serve warm or at room temperature. *Makes 8 servings*

NUTRIENTS PER SERVING (1 triangle): Carbohydrate: 9 g, Fat: 2 g, Protein: 3 g, Calories: 62 (26% of calories from fat), Saturated Fat: 1 g, Sodium: 142 mg

Lemon and Fennel Marinated Vegetables

1 cup water
2 medium carrots, cut diagonally into ½-inch-thick slices
1 cup small whole fresh mushrooms
1 small red or green bell pepper, cored, seeded and cut into ¾-inch pieces
3 tablespoons lemon juice
1 tablespoon sugar
1 tablespoon olive oil
1 clove garlic, minced
½ teaspoon fennel seeds, crushed
½ teaspoon dried basil leaves, crushed
¼ teaspoon black pepper

1. Bring water to a boil over high heat in small saucepan. Add carrots. Return to a boil. Reduce heat to medium-low. Cover and simmer about 5 minutes or until carrots are crisp-tender. Drain and cool.

2. Place carrots, mushrooms and bell pepper in large resealable plastic food storage bag. Combine lemon juice, sugar, oil, garlic, fennel seeds, basil and black pepper in small bowl. Pour over vegetables. Close bag securely; turn to coat. Marinate in refrigerator 8 to 24 hours, turning occasionally.

3. Drain vegetables; discard marinade. Place vegetables in serving dish.

Makes 4 servings

NUTRIENTS PER SERVING (¼ of total recipe): Carbohydrate: 9 g, Fat: 1 g, Protein: 1 g, Calories: 47 (24% of calories from fat), Saturated Fat: <1 g, Sodium: 15 mg

Lemon and Fennel Marinated Vegetables

Mexican Slaw

1 corn tortilla, cut into thin strips
   Nonstick cooking spray
¼ teaspoon chili powder
3 cups shredded green cabbage
1 cup shredded red cabbage
½ cup shredded carrots
½ cup sliced radishes
½ cup corn kernels
¼ cup coarsely chopped cilantro
¼ cup mayonnaise
1 tablespoon lime juice
2 teaspoons vinegar
1 teaspoon honey
½ teaspoon cumin
¼ teaspoon salt
¼ teaspoon black pepper

1. Preheat oven to 350°F. Arrange tortilla strips in even layer on nonstick baking sheet. Spray strips with nonstick cooking spray; sprinkle with chili powder. Bake 6 to 8 minutes or until strips are crisp. set aside.

2. Place all remaining ingredients in a large bowl, tossing and stirring to evenly distribute ingredients. Serve with baked tortilla strips. *Makes 8 servings*

NUTRIENTS PER SERVING (⅛ of total recipe): Carbohydrate: 8 g, Fat: 6 g, Protein: 1 g, Calories: 83 (59% of calories from fat), Saturated Fat: <1 g, Sodium: 129 mg

Cool and Creamy Pea Salad

2 tablespoons finely chopped red onion
1 tablespoon reduced-fat mayonnaise
$\frac{1}{8}$ teaspoon salt
$\frac{1}{8}$ teaspoon black pepper
$\frac{1}{2}$ cup frozen green peas, thawed
$\frac{1}{4}$ cup diced red bell pepper
$\frac{1}{4}$ cup diced cucumber

1. Combine onion, mayonnaise, salt and pepper in medium bowl; stir until well blended.

2. Add remaining ingredients and toss gently to coat.   *Makes 2 servings*

NUTRIENTS PER SERVING ($\frac{1}{2}$ cup salad): Carbohydrate: 8 g, Fat: 3 g, Protein: 2 g, Calories: 65 (36% of calories from fat), Saturated Fat: 1 g, Sodium: 238 mg

Garlic Greens

5 to 6 ounces spinach
1 tablespoon reduced-fat margarine or olive oil
4 cloves garlic, minced

1. Wash spinach; remove and discard stems. Melt margarine in small skillet over medium heat. Add garlic; cook and stir about 1 minute. Do not allow garlic brown.

2. Add spinach to skillet; stir to coat with garlic. Cover; cook 1 minute or until spinach is wilted. Serve immediately.   *Makes 2 servings*

NUTRIENTS PER SERVING ($\frac{2}{3}$ cup): Carbohydrate: 5 g, Fat: 4 g, Protein: 3 g, Calories: 58 (52% of calories from fat), Saturated Fat: <1 g, Sodium: 133 mg

Fresh Greens with Hot Bacon Dressing

3 cups torn spinach leaves
3 cups torn romaine lettuce
2 small tomatoes, cut into wedges
1 cup sliced mushrooms
1 medium carrot, shredded
1 slice bacon, cut into small pieces
3 tablespoons red wine vinegar
1 tablespoon water
¼ teaspoon dried tarragon, crushed
⅛ teaspoon coarsely ground pepper
2 teaspoons EQUAL® SPOONFUL*

May substitute 1 packet EQUAL® sweetener.

• Combine spinach, romaine, tomatoes, mushrooms and carrot in large bowl; set aside.

• Cook bacon in 12-inch skillet until crisp. Carefully stir in vinegar, water, tarragon and pepper. Heat to boiling; remove from heat. Stir in Equal®.

• Add spinach mixture to skillet. Toss 30 to 60 seconds or just until greens are wilted. Transfer to serving bowl. Serve immediately.   *Makes 4 to 6 servings*

NUTRIENTS PER SERVING (1⅓ cups): Carbohydrate: 9 g, Fat: 1 g, Protein: 3 g, Calories: 51 (18% of calories from fat), Saturated Fat: <1 g, Sodium: 74 mg

Fresh Greens with Hot Bacon Dressing

Grilled Chicken au Poivre Salad

    4 boneless skinless chicken breasts (about 1¼ pounds)
  ¼ cup finely chopped onion
2½ tablespoons white wine vinegar, divided
  ¼ cup plus 3 tablespoons olive oil, divided
   2 teaspoons cracked or coarse ground black pepper
  ½ teaspoon salt
  ¼ teaspoon poultry seasoning
   3 cloves garlic, minced
   1 tablespoon Dijon mustard
    Dash sugar
   1 bag (10 ounces) prewashed salad greens
   2 cherry tomatoes, halved

1. Place chicken, onion, 1 tablespoon vinegar, ¼ cup oil, pepper, salt, poultry seasoning and garlic in resealable plastic food storage bag. Seal bag; knead to coat chicken. Refrigerate at least 2 hours or overnight.

2. Grill chicken on covered grill over medium-hot coals 10 to 15 minutes or until chicken is no longer pink in center.

3. For dressing, combine remaining 1½ tablespoons vinegar, 3 tablespoons oil, mustard and sugar in small bowl; whisk until smooth.

4. Arrange salad greens and cherry tomatoes on 4 plates.

5. Cut chicken crosswise into strips. Arrange strips on top of greens. Drizzle with dressing.

Makes 4 servings

NUTRIENTS PER SERVING (¼ of total recipe): Carbohydrate: 5 g, Fat: 15 g, Protein: 23 g, Calories: 252 (55% of calories from fat), Saturated Fat: 2 g, Sodium: 439 mg

Grilled Chicken au Poivre Salad

Garden Greens With Fennel Dressing

Dressing

$\frac{1}{2}$ teaspoon unflavored gelatin

2 tablespoons cold water

$\frac{1}{4}$ cup boiling water

$\frac{1}{2}$ teaspoon salt

$\frac{1}{2}$ teaspoon sugar

$\frac{1}{4}$ cup raspberry or wine vinegar

1 tablespoon fresh lemon juice

$\frac{1}{4}$ teaspoon dry mustard

$\frac{1}{4}$ teaspoon ground fennel seeds or anise extract

$\frac{1}{8}$ teaspoon black pepper

$1\frac{1}{4}$ teaspoons walnut or canola oil

Salad

1 head (10 ounces) Bibb lettuce, washed and torn into bite-size pieces

1 head (10 ounces) radicchio, washed and torn into bite-size pieces

1 bunch arugula (3 ounces), washed and torn into bite-size pieces

1 cup mâche or spinach leaves, washed and torn into bite-size pieces

1 fennel bulb (8 ounces), finely chopped

1 tablespoon pine nuts, toasted

1. To prepare dressing, sprinkle gelatin over cold water in small bowl; let stand 1 minute to soften. Add boiling water; stir 2 minutes or until gelatin is completely dissolved. Add salt and sugar; stir until sugar is completely dissolved. Add all remaining dressing ingredients except oil; mix well. Slowly whisk in oil until well blended. Cover and refrigerate 2 hours or overnight. Shake well before using.

2. To prepare salad, place all salad ingredients except pine nuts in large bowl. Add dressing; toss until well coated. Divide salad among 6 chilled salad plates. Top each salad with $\frac{1}{2}$ teaspoon pine nuts. *Makes 6 servings*

NUTRIENTS PER SERVING ($\frac{1}{6}$ of total recipe): Carbohydrate: 9 g, Fat: 2 g, Protein: 3 g, Calories: 60 (30% of calories from fat), Saturated Fat: <1 g, Sodium: 226 mg

Crunchy Asparagus

1 package (10 ounces) frozen asparagus cuts
1 teaspoon lemon juice
3 to 4 drops hot pepper sauce
$\frac{1}{4}$ teaspoon salt (optional)
$\frac{1}{4}$ teaspoon dried basil leaves, crushed
$\frac{1}{8}$ teaspoon black pepper
2 teaspoons sunflower kernels
Lemon slices (optional)

Microwave Directions

1. Place asparagus and 2 tablespoons water in 1-quart microwavable casserole dish; cover. Microwave at HIGH $4\frac{1}{2}$ to $5\frac{1}{2}$ minutes or until asparagus is hot, stirring after half the cooking time to break apart. Drain. Cover; set aside.

2. Combine lemon juice, hot pepper sauce, salt, basil and pepper in small bowl. Pour mixture over asparagus; toss to coat. Sprinkle with sunflower kernels. Garnish with lemon slices, if desired.   *Makes 4 servings*

NUTRIENTS PER SERVING ($\frac{1}{4}$ of total recipe): Carbohydrate: 4 g, Fat: 1 g, Protein: 2 g, Calories: 29 (27% of calories from fat), Saturated Fat: <1 g, Sodium: 4 mg

Marinated Tomato Salad

Marinade

1½ cups tarragon or white wine vinegar
½ teaspoon salt
¼ cup finely chopped shallots
2 tablespoons finely chopped chives
2 tablespoons fresh lemon juice
¼ teaspoon white pepper
2 tablespoons extra-virgin olive oil

Salad

6 plum tomatoes, quartered vertically
2 large yellow tomatoes,* sliced horizontally into ½-inch slices
16 red cherry tomatoes, halved vertically
16 small yellow pear tomatoes,* halved vertically

Substitute 10 plum tomatoes, quartered vertically, for yellow tomatoes and yellow pear tomatoes, if desired.

1. To prepare marinade, combine vinegar and salt in large bowl; stir until salt is completely dissolved. Add shallots, chives, lemon juice and pepper; mix well. Slowly whisk in oil until well blended.

2. Add tomatoes to marinade; toss well. Cover; let stand at room temperature 2 to 3 hours.

Makes 8 servings

NUTRIENTS PER SERVING (⅛ of total recipe): Carbohydrate: 9 g, Fat: 4 g,
Protein: 2 g, Calories: 72 (45% of calories from fat), Saturated Fat: <1 g, Sodium: 163 mg

Marinated Tomato Salad

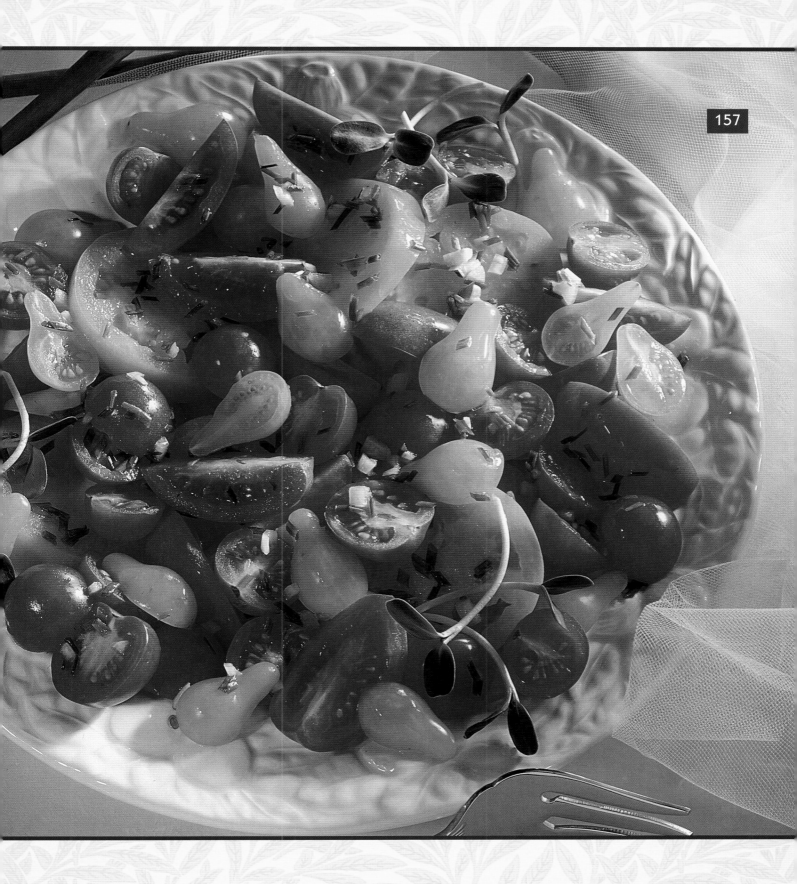

Herbed Mushroom Vegetable Medley

4 ounces button or crimini mushrooms
1 medium red or yellow bell pepper, cut into ¼-inch-wide strips
1 medium zucchini, cut crosswise into ¼-inch-thick slices
1 medium yellow squash, cut crosswise into ¼-inch-thick slices
3 tablespoons butter or margarine, melted
1 tablespoon chopped fresh thyme *or* 1 teaspoon dried thyme leaves
1 tablespoon chopped fresh basil *or* 1 teaspoon dried basil leaves
1 tablespoon chopped fresh chives or green onion tops
1 clove garlic, minced
¼ teaspoon salt
¼ teaspoon black pepper

1. Prepare grill for direct cooking.

2. Cut thin slice from base of mushroom stems with paring knife; discard. Thinly slice mushroom stems and caps. Combine mushrooms, bell pepper, zucchini and squash in large bowl. Combine butter, thyme, basil, chives, garlic, salt and black pepper in small bowl. Pour over vegetable mixture; toss to coat well.

3. Transfer mixture to 20×14-inch sheet of heavy-duty foil; wrap, leaving head space for heat circulation. Place foil packet on grid. Grill on covered grill over medium coals 20 to 25 minutes or until vegetables are fork-tender. Open packet carefully to serve.

Makes 4 to 6 servings

NUTRIENTS PER SERVING (⅔ cup): Carbohydrate: 5 g, Fat: 9 g, Protein: 2 g, Calories: 106 (76% of calories from fat), Saturated Fat: 6 g, Sodium: 247 mg

Herbed Mushroom Vegetable Medley

Garlic Lovers' Chicken Caesar Salad

Dressing

1 can (10¾ ounces) reduced-fat condensed cream of chicken soup, undiluted
½ cup fat-free reduced-sodium chicken broth
¼ cup balsamic vinegar
¼ cup fat-free grated Parmesan cheese, divided
3 cloves garlic, minced
1 tablespoon reduced-sodium Worcestershire sauce
¼ teaspoon black pepper

Salad

2 heads romaine lettuce, torn into 2-inch pieces
4 grilled boneless skinless chicken breasts (about 1 pound), cut into 2-inch strips
½ cup fat-free herb-seasoned croutons

1. Combine soup, broth, vinegar, 2 tablespoons cheese, garlic, Worcestershire sauce and pepper in food processor or blender; process until smooth.

2. Combine lettuce and 1 cup dressing in large salad bowl; toss well to coat. Reserve remaining dressing for another use. Top with chicken and croutons; sprinkle with remaining 2 tablespoons cheese.   *Makes 8 servings*

NUTRIENTS PER SERVING (1¼ cups lettuce mixture with about 4 chicken strips, 1 tablespoon croutons and ¾ teaspoon cheese): Carbohydrate: 10 g, Fat: 2 g, Protein: 17 g, Calories: 132 (15% of calories from fat), Saturated Fat: 1 g, Sodium: 185 mg

Garlic Lovers' Chicken Caesar Salad

Creamed Spinach

3 cups water
2 bags (10 ounces each) fresh spinach, washed, stems removed and leaves chopped
2 teaspoons margarine
2 tablespoons all-purpose flour
1 cup fat-free (skim) milk
2 tablespoons grated Parmesan cheese
⅛ teaspoon white pepper
   Ground nutmeg

1. Bring water to a boil; add spinach. Reduce heat and simmer, covered, about 5 minutes or until spinach is wilted. Drain well. Set aside.

2. Melt margarine in small saucepan. Stir in flour; cook over medium-low heat 1 minute, stirring constantly. Using wire whisk, stir in milk; bring to a boil. Cook, whisking constantly, 1 to 2 minutes or until mixture thickens. Stir in cheese and pepper.

3. Stir spinach into sauce; heat thoroughly. Spoon into serving bowl; sprinkle lightly with nutmeg. Garnish as desired.   *Makes 4 servings*

NUTRIENTS PER SERVING (¼ of total recipe): Carbohydrate: 10 g, Fat: 3 g, Protein: 7 g, Calories: 91 (30% of calories from fat), Saturated Fat: 1 g, Sodium: 188 mg

Creamed Spinach

Latino Slaw

Prep Time: 15 minutes

- ¼ **cup jarred jalapeños**
- 2 **cloves garlic**
- 1 **tablespoon ground cumin**
- 1 **tablespoon fresh oregano leaves**
- 3 **tablespoons olive oil**
  Juice of 1 lime
- 1 **teaspoon salt**
- 1 **cup CARB OPTIONS™ Whipped Dressing**
- 6 **cups thinly sliced Napa cabbage**
- 1 **red onion, halved and thinly sliced**
- ½ **cup chopped fresh cilantro**

1. In a blender, process jalapeños, garlic, cumin, oregano, olive oil, lime juice, salt and Carb Options Whipped Dressing 30 seconds or until smooth; set aside.

2. In a large bowl, combine the cabbage, onion and cilantro. Add the dressing mixture and toss well. Let stand 20 minutes before serving.   *Makes 6 servings*

NUTRIENTS PER SERVING (1 cup): Carbohydrate: 7 g, Fat: 8 g, Protein: 2 g, Calories: 100 (72% of calories from fat), Saturated Fat: 1 g, Sodium: 500 mg

Italian Grilled Vegetables

Prep Time: 10 minutes   *Marinate Time:* 15 minutes   *Cook Time:* 15 minutes

3 pounds assorted fresh vegetables*
1 cup CARB OPTIONS™ Italian Dressing

Use any combination of the following, thickly sliced: eggplant, zucchini, yellow squash or large mushrooms.

1. In large, shallow nonaluminum baking dish or plastic bag, toss vegetables with Carb Options Italian Dressing. Cover, or close bag, and marinate in refrigerator, 15 minutes to 1 hour, turning once.

2. Remove vegetables from marinade, reserving marinade. Grill or broil vegetables, turning and basting occasionally with reserved marinade, until vegetables are tender.

Makes 8 servings

NUTRIENTS PER SERVING (⅛ of total recipe): Carbohydrate: 8 g, Fat: 9 g, Protein: 2 g, Calories: 110 (74% of calories from fat), Saturated Fat: 2 g, Sodium: 370 mg

Broccoli with Cheddar Sauce

Prep Time: 10 minutes   *Cook Time:* 5 minutes

1 cup CARB OPTIONS™ Double Cheddar Sauce
1 bag (16 ounces) frozen broccoli spears, cooked

In 1-quart saucepan, heat Carb Options Double Cheddar Sauce. To serve, pour over hot broccoli.

Makes 4 servings

NUTRIENTS PER SERVING (¼ of total recipe): Carbohydrate: 8 g, Fat: 9 g, Protein: 6 g, Calories: 120 (68% of calories from fat), Saturated Fat: 3 g, Sodium: 510 mg

The Best for Last

Speedy Pineapple-Lime Sorbet

1 ripe pineapple, cut into cubes (about 4 cups)
1/3 cup frozen limeade concentrate, thawed
1 to 2 tablespoons fresh lime juice
1 teaspoon grated lime peel

1. Arrange pineapple in single layer on large baking pan; freeze at least 1 hour or until very firm.

2. Combine frozen pineapple, limeade, lime juice and lime peel in food processor; process until smooth and fluffy. If pineapple doesn't become smooth and fluffy, let stand 30 minutes to soften slightly; repeat processing. Garnish as desired. Serve immediately.

Makes 8 servings

Note: This dessert is best if served immediately, but it can be made ahead, stored in the freezer and then softened several minutes before being served.

NUTRIENTS PER SERVING (1/2 cup sorbet): Carbohydrate: 15 g, Fat: <1 g, Protein: <1 g, Calories: 56 (5% of calories from fat), Saturated Fat: <1 g, Sodium: 1 mg

The Best for Last

168

Chocolate Fondue with Fresh Fruit

3 tablespoons unsweetened cocoa powder
1 cup heavy cream, divided
4 ounces (½ cup) cream cheese, cut in chunks
3 tablespoons plus 1 teaspoon sucralose-based sugar substitute
½ teaspoon vanilla
24 green or red seedless grapes
12 small to medium strawberries, halved, *or* 6 large strawberries quartered

1. Combine cocoa with ½ cup cream in small saucepan or fondue pot over low heat; whisk to mix completely. When cocoa mixture is hot and thick, add remaining cream and cream cheese. Cook, stirring constantly, until mixture is smooth and thick. Add sucralose and vanilla; stir to mix.

2. Keep fondue warm over very low heat. Arrange strawberries and grapes on a plate. Use wooden skewers or fondue forks for dipping.   *Makes 8 servings*

Note: Substitute fruit in season for the grapes and strawberries.

NUTRIENTS PER SERVING (6 pieces fruit plus 3 tablespoons fondue):
Carbohydrate: 7 g, Fat: 16 g, Protein: 2 g, Calories: 177 (80% of calories from fat), Saturated Fat: 10 g, Sodium: 55 mg

Chocolate Fondue with Fresh Fruit

Café au Lait Ice Cream Sundae

3 cups whipping cream, divided
4 egg yolks, lightly beaten
1 tablespoon instant coffee granules
½ cup plus 2 tablespoons no-calorie sugar substitute for baking, divided
½ teaspoon vanilla
½ cup chopped walnuts or pecans

1. Pour 2 cups cream into medium saucepan. Whisk egg yolks and coffee granules into cream. Heat 10 minutes over low heat, stirring constantly, until mixture reaches 160°F. Mixture will thicken as it cooks.

2. Pour mixture into bowl; stir in ½ cup sugar substitute until well blended. Refrigerate until cold, about 2 to 3 hours. Pour chilled mixture into ice cream maker; process according to manufacturer's directions.

3. Whip remaining 1 cup cream, 2 tablespoons sugar substitute and vanilla until stiff. Scoop ice cream into serving bowls; top with whipped cream. Sprinkle with nuts just before serving.
Makes 4 servings

Tip: The ice cream will become harder the longer it is stored in freezer, so it is best eaten when freshly made.

NUTRIENTS PER SERVING (¼ of total recipe): Carbohydrate: 12 g, Fat: 82 g, Protein: 9 g, Calories: 798 (92% of calories from fat), Saturated Fat: 44 g, Sodium: 79 mg

Café au Lait Ice Cream Sundae

Chocolate-Caramel S'Mores

12 chocolate wafer cookies or chocolate graham cracker squares
2 tablespoons fat-free caramel topping
6 large marshmallows

1. Prepare coals for grilling. Place 6 wafer cookies top down on plate. Spread 1 teaspoon caramel topping in center of each wafer to within about ¼ inch of edge.

2. Spear 1 to 2 marshmallows onto long wood-handled skewer. Hold several inches above coals 3 to 5 minutes or until marshmallows are golden and very soft, turning slowly. Push 1 marshmallow off into center of caramel. Top with plain wafer. Repeat with remaining marshmallows and wafers.

Makes 6 servings

NUTRIENTS PER SERVING (1 s'more): Carbohydrate: 14 g, Fat: 2 g, Protein: 1 g, Calories: 72 (23% of calories from fat), Saturated Fat: 1 g, Sodium: 77 mg

Chocolate-Caramel S'Mores

Easy Fruit Tarts

Prep Time: 20 minutes   *Bake Time:* 5 minutes

12 wonton skins
   Vegetable cooking spray
2 tablespoons apple jelly or apricot fruit spread
1½ cups sliced or cut-up fruit such as DOLE® Bananas, Strawberries or Red or Green Seedless Grapes
1 cup nonfat or low fat yogurt, any flavor

• Press wonton skins into 12 muffin cups sprayed with vegetable cooking spray, allowing corners to stand up over edges of muffin cups.

• Bake at 375°F 5 minutes or until lightly browned. Carefully remove wonton cups to wire rack; cool.

• Cook and stir jelly in small saucepan over low heat until jelly melts.

• Brush bottoms of cooled wonton cups with melted jelly. Place two fruit slices in each cup; spoon rounded tablespoon of yogurt on top of fruit. Garnish with fruit slice and mint leaves. Serve immediately.   *Makes 12 servings*

NUTRIENTS PER SERVING (1 fruit tart): Carbohydrate: 12 g, Fat: <1 g, Protein: 1 g, Calories: 57 (5% of calories from fat), Saturated Fat: <1 g, Sodium: 32 mg

Chocolate-Almond Meringue Puffs

2 tablespoons granulated sugar
3 packets sugar substitute
1½ teaspoons unsweetened cocoa powder
2 egg whites, at room temperature
½ teaspoon vanilla
¼ teaspoon cream of tartar
¼ teaspoon almond extract
⅛ teaspoon salt
1½ ounces sliced almonds
3 tablespoons sugar-free seedless raspberry fruit spread

1. Preheat oven to 275°F. Combine granulated sugar, sugar substitute and cocoa in small bowl; set aside.

2. Place egg whites in small bowl; beat at high speed of electric mixer until foamy. Add vanilla, cream of tartar, almond extract and salt; beat until soft peaks form. Add sugar mixture, 1 tablespoon at a time, beating until stiff peaks form.

3. Line baking sheet with foil. Spoon 15 equal mounds of egg white mixture onto foil. Sprinkle with almonds.

4. Bake 1 hour. Turn oven off but do not open door. Leave puffs in oven 2 hours longer or until completely dry. Remove from oven; cool completely.

5. Stir fruit spread and spoon about ½ teaspoon onto each meringue just before serving.

Makes 15 servings

Tip: Puffs are best if eaten the same day they're made. If necessary, store in an airtight container, adding fruit topping at time of serving.

NUTRIENTS PER SERVING (1 puff): Carbohydrate: 5 g, Fat: 1 g, Protein: 1 g, Calories: 36 (36% of calories from fat), Saturated Fat: <1 g, Sodium: 27 mg

Chocolate-Almond Meringue Puffs

Strawberry-Topped Cheesecake Cups

1 cup sliced strawberries
10 packages sugar substitute, divided
1 teaspoon vanilla, divided
½ teaspoon grated orange peel
¼ teaspoon grated fresh ginger
1 package (8 ounces) cream cheese, softened
½ cup sour cream
2 tablespoons granulated sugar
16 vanilla wafers, crushed

1. Combine strawberries, 1 package sugar substitute, ¼ teaspoon vanilla, orange peel and ginger in medium bowl; toss gently. Let stand 20 minutes to allow flavors to blend.

2. Meanwhile, combine cream cheese, sour cream, remaining 9 packets sugar substitute and granulated sugar in medium mixing bowl. Add remaining ¾ teaspoon vanilla; beat 30 seconds at low speed of electric mixer. Increase to medium speed; beat 30 seconds or until smooth.

3. Spoon cream cheese mixture into 8 individual ¼-cup ramekins. Top each with about 2 tablespoons vanilla wafer crumbs and about 2 tablespoons strawberry mixture.

Makes 8 servings

NUTRIENTS PER SERVING (⅛ of total recipe): Carbohydrate: 15 g, Fat: 15 g, Protein: 3 g, Calories: 205 (66% of calories from fat), Saturated Fat: 9 g, Sodium: 127 mg

Strawberry-Topped Cheesecake Cups

Fruit Freezies

1½ cups (12 ounces) canned or thawed frozen peach slices, drained
¾ cup peach nectar
1 tablespoon sugar
¼ to ½ teaspoon coconut extract (optional)

1. Place peaches, nectar, sugar and extract in food processor or blender container; process until smooth.

2. Spoon 2 tablespoons fruit mixture into each mold of ice cube tray.*

3. Freeze until almost firm. Insert frill pick into each cube; freeze until firm.

Makes 12 servings

Or, pour ⅓ cup fruit mixture into each of 8 plastic pop molds or small paper or plastic cups. Freeze until almost firm. Insert wooden stick into each mold; freeze until firm.

Apricot Freezies: Substitute canned apricot halves for peach slices and apricot nectar for peach nectar.

Pear Freezies: Substitute canned pear slices for peach slices, pear nectar for peach nectar and almond extract for coconut extract.

Pineapple Freezies: Substitute crushed pineapple for peach slices and unsweetened pineapple juice for peach nectar.

Mango Freezies: Substitute chopped fresh mango for peach slices and mango nectar for peach nectar. Omit coconut extract.

NUTRIENTS PER SERVING (2 freezies): Carbohydrate: 5 g, Fat: <1 g, Protein: <1 g, Calories: 19 (1% of calories from fat), Saturated Fat: <1 g, Sodium: 2 mg

Easy Raspberry Ice Cream

8 ounces (1¾ cups) frozen unsweetened raspberries
2 to 3 tablespoons powdered sugar
½ cup whipping cream

1. Place raspberries in food processor fitted with steel blade. Process using on/off pulsing action about 15 seconds or until raspberries resemble coarse crumbs.

2. Add sugar; process using on/off pulsing action until smooth. With processor running, add cream, processing until well blended. Serve immediately.   *Makes 3 servings*

NUTRIENTS PER SERVING (⅓ of total recipe): Carbohydrate: 15 g, Fat: 15 g, Protein: 2 g, Calories: 193 (68% of calories from fat), Saturated Fat: 9 g, Sodium: 15 mg

Peanutty Ricotta Mousse

Prep Time: 5 minutes

½ cup part-skim ricotta cheese
1½ tablespoons CARB OPTIONS™ Creamy Peanut Spread
1 teaspoon SPLENDA® No Calorie Sweetener
Dash ground cinnamon

In small bowl, blend cheese, Carb Options Creamy Peanut Spread and sweetener. To serve, sprinkle with cinnamon. Chill, if desired.   *Makes 1 serving*

Variation: For a Chocolate Peanutty Ricotta Mousse, stir in ½ teaspoon unsweetened cocoa powder and an additional ½ teaspoon sweetener.

NUTRIENTS PER SERVING (½ cup): Carbohydrate: 10 g, Fat: 20 g, Protein: 19 g, Calories: 290 (62% of calories from fat), Saturated Fat: 8 g, Sodium: 240 mg

Easy Raspberry Ice Cream

Low-Carb Cream Cheese Dessert

2 packages (8 ounces each) cream cheese, softened
2 teaspoons vanilla, divided
1 package (4-serving size) sugar-free lime-flavored gelatin
15 packets sugar substitute, divided
¾ cup hot water
2 cups heavy whipping cream, divided

1. Beat cream cheese and 1 teaspoon vanilla in large bowl with electric mixer. Combine gelatin and 11 packets sugar substitute in small bowl. Pour in hot water; stir until dissolved.

2. Add gelatin mixture to cream cheese mixture. Beat at low speed until well combined.

3. Beat 1 cup whipping cream in medium bowl until stiff peaks form. Add to cream cheese mixture. Beat at low speed. Pour mixture into 8×8-inch pan. Chill 2 hours.

4. Before serving, beat remaining 1 cup whipping cream, 1 teaspoon vanilla and 4 packets sugar substitute in medium bowl with electric mixer until stiff peaks form. Place dollop of whipped cream mixture on each serving of dessert. *Makes 8 servings*

NUTRIENTS PER SERVING (⅛ of total recipe): Carbohydrate: 5 g, Fat: 42 g, Protein: 6 g, Calories: 420 (89% of calories from fat), Saturated Fat: 26 g, Sodium: 221 mg

Cranberry-Orange Bread Pudding

2 cups cubed cinnamon bread
¼ cup dried cranberries
2 cups low-fat (1%) milk
1 package (4-serving size) sugar-free cook-and-serve vanilla pudding
    and pie filling mix*
½ cup cholesterol-free egg substitute
1 teaspoon vanilla
1 teaspoon grated orange peel
½ teaspoon ground cinnamon
    Low-fat no-sugar-added vanilla ice cream (optional)

*Do not use instant pudding and pie filling.

1. Preheat oven to 325°F. Spray 9 custard cups with nonstick cooking spray.

2. Evenly divide bread cubes among custard cups. Bake 10 minutes; add cranberries.

3. Combine remaining ingredients except ice cream in medium bowl. Carefully pour over mixture in custard cups. Let stand 5 to 10 minutes.

4. Place cups on baking sheet; bake 25 to 30 minutes or until centers are almost set. Let stand 10 minutes. Serve with ice cream, if desired.   *Makes 9 servings*

NUTRIENTS PER SERVING (1 custard cup pudding without ice cream):
Carbohydrate: 11 g, Fat: 1 g, Protein: 4 g, Calories: 67 (13% of calories from fat), Saturated Fat: <1 g, Sodium: 190 mg

The publisher would like to thank the companies and organizations listed below for the use of their recipes and photographs in this publication.

Birds Eye®

Butterball® Turkey

Del Monte Corporation

Dole Food Company, Inc.

Egg Beaters®

Equal® sweetener

Hormel Foods, LLC

The Kingsford Products Company

National Fisheries Institute

The J.M. Smucker Company

Uncle Ben's Inc.

Unilever Bestfoods North America

METRIC CONVERSION CHART

VOLUME MEASUREMENTS (dry)

1/8 teaspoon = 0.5 mL
1/4 teaspoon = 1 mL
1/2 teaspoon = 2 mL
3/4 teaspoon = 4 mL
1 teaspoon = 5 mL
1 tablespoon = 15 mL
2 tablespoons = 30 mL
1/4 cup = 60 mL
1/3 cup = 75 mL
1/2 cup = 125 mL
2/3 cup = 150 mL
3/4 cup = 175 mL
1 cup = 250 mL
2 cups = 1 pint = 500 mL
3 cups = 750 mL
4 cups = 1 quart = 1 L

VOLUME MEASUREMENTS (fluid)

1 fluid ounce (2 tablespoons) = 30 mL
4 fluid ounces (1/2 cup) = 125 mL
8 fluid ounces (1 cup) = 250 mL
12 fluid ounces (1 1/2 cups) = 375 mL
16 fluid ounces (2 cups) = 500 mL

WEIGHTS (mass)

1/2 ounce = 15 g
1 ounce = 30 g
3 ounces = 90 g
4 ounces = 120 g
8 ounces = 225 g
10 ounces = 285 g
12 ounces = 360 g
16 ounces = 1 pound = 450 g

DIMENSIONS

1/16 inch = 2 mm
1/8 inch = 3 mm
1/4 inch = 6 mm
1/2 inch = 1.5 cm
3/4 inch = 2 cm
1 inch = 2.5 cm

OVEN TEMPERATURES

250°F = 120°C
275°F = 140°C
300°F = 150°C
325°F = 160°C
350°F = 180°C
375°F = 190°C
400°F = 200°C
425°F = 220°C
450°F = 230°C

BAKING PAN SIZES

Utensil	Size in Inches/Quarts	Metric Volume	Size in Centimeters
Baking or Cake Pan (square or rectangular)	8 × 8 × 2	2 L	20 × 20 × 5
	9 × 9 × 2	2.5 L	23 × 23 × 5
	12 × 8 × 2	3 L	30 × 20 × 5
	13 × 9 × 2	3.5 L	33 × 23 × 5
Loaf Pan	8 × 4 × 3	1.5 L	20 × 10 × 7
	9 × 5 × 3	2 L	23 × 13 × 7
Round Layer Cake Pan	8 × 1½	1.2 L	20 × 4
	9 × 1½	1.5 L	23 × 4
Pie Plate	8 × 1¼	750 mL	20 × 3
	9 × 1¼	1 L	23 × 3
Baking Dish or Casserole	1 quart	1 L	—
	1½ quart	1.5 L	—
	2 quart	2 L	—